Industrial Leaders

Industrial Leaders

Economic Powerhouses Explained

Ehsan Sheroy

UNIEK ENTERPRISES

CONTENTS

INDEX

Chapter 7: Globalization and Trade

Chapter 8: Challenges and Future Outlook

1

Chapter 1

Introduction to Industrial Leaders

The universe of industry has forever been set apart by pioneers who have molded the course of human advancement. These modern chiefs, frequently visionaries and trailblazers, play had a critical impact in the development and change of economies, innovation, and society. Their commitments have upset their particular fields as well as left an enduring effect on the manner in which we live, work, and connect with our general surroundings. In this investigation of modern pioneers, we will dig into the lives and traditions of the absolute most persuasive figures in history who have made a permanent imprint on their businesses and, as a rule, on the world overall.

One of the earliest instances of modern authority can be found in the existence of James Watt, whose spearheading work in steam motor innovation in the eighteenth century established the groundwork for the Modern Unrest. Watt's upgrades to the steam motor made it a more proficient and viable wellspring of force, prompting a significant change in assembling, transportation, and energy creation. His developments introduced another time of industrialization that saw the ascent of production lines and the automation of already manual assignments, everlastingly having an impact on how merchandise were delivered and appropriated.

As we push ahead in time, we experience another famous modern pioneer, Thomas Edison. Frequently alluded to as "The Wizard of Menlo Park," Edison was a productive creator with north of 1,000 licenses in his possession. He is most popular for his commitments to the improvement of the electric light, phonograph, and movies, among numerous others. Edison's tenacious quest for advancement and his capacity to transform his thoughts into pragmatic, attractive items epitomize the pioneering soul that has driven incalculable modern pioneers.

Henry Passage, the pioneer behind the Portage Engine Organization, is another figure who poses a potential threat in the chronicles of modern history. His vision of reasonable cars for the majority reformed the car business and, likewise, meaningfully impacted the manner in which individuals live and work. Passage's presentation of the sequential construction system creation technique expanded effectiveness as well as set another norm for assembling that would be taken on across different ventures.

Moving into the domain of data innovation, the name Steve Occupations promptly rings a bell. Prime supporter of Mac Inc., Occupations was a genuine visionary who had an uncanny capacity to foresee and shape purchaser wants.

His administration not just brought us famous items like the iPhone, iPad, and MacBook yet additionally changed the manner in which we cooperate with innovation. The idea of easy to understand plan and the consistent reconciliation of equipment and programming were signs of Occupations' way to deal with item improvement.

While these verifiable figures give us a brief look at the effect of modern pioneers, it is fundamental to perceive that modern initiative isn't restricted to the past. In the contemporary world, another age of modern pioneers has arisen, molding ventures as different as web based business, sustainable power, and space investigation.

Take Jeff Bezos, the pioneer behind Amazon, for example. Bezos transformed an internet based book shop into a worldwide online business realm that has upset customary retail and meaningfully had an impact on the manner in which we shop. His accentuation on client centricity and long haul thinking has been a principal quality of Amazon's prosperity.

Elon Musk, then again, has become inseparable from development in the electric vehicle and aviation ventures. As the President of Tesla and SpaceX, Musk has pushed the limits of what is conceivable in the two areas. His aggressive objectives of colonizing Mars and speeding up the progress to feasible energy show the nervy vision that frequently portrays modern pioneers.

In the domain of sustainable power, we find the case of Greta Thunberg, a youthful ecological dissident who has energized worldwide thoughtfulness regarding the earnest requirement for environment activity. While not a customary modern forerunner in that frame of mind of industry icons, her impact in pushing for supportable practices and considering world pioneers responsible for their ecological strategies can't be put into words.

As we set out on this investigation of modern pioneers, it is fundamental to comprehend what separates them and what characteristics and qualities are normal among them. Administration in the modern world is complex and can appear in different structures. Nonetheless, there are a few critical qualities and qualities that will more often than not characterize modern pioneers:

Vision: Modern pioneers have an unmistakable and convincing vision representing things to come. They see open doors and potential outcomes that others might disregard, and they can verbalize and impart this vision successfully.

Advancement: Development is at the center of modern initiative. These pioneers are frequently disruptors, presenting new innovations, plans of action, or items that change the state of affairs and make an upper hand.

Steadiness: Modern pioneers face various difficulties and misfortunes. Their capacity to drive forward notwithstanding misfortune is a typical quality. Whether it's refining an item, defeating market opposition, or exploring administrative obstacles, they are strong in their quest for progress.

Risk-taking: Modern pioneers are not unwilling to proceeding with well balanced plans of action. They comprehend that advancement frequently includes wandering into an unfamiliar area and that some degree of hazard is intrinsic in pushing the limits of what is conceivable.

Versatility: In a quickly impacting world, flexibility is significant. Modern pioneers are adaptable and open to changing their procedures and approaches as conditions advance. They can turn when essential while remaining consistent with their general vision.

Energy and Responsibility: These pioneers are profoundly energetic about their work. Their obligation to their vision and the effect they need to make drives them to contribute time, energy, and assets into their undertakings.

Compassion: Compelling modern pioneers grasp the requirements and wants of their clients or partners. They stand by listening to criticism, focus on client experience, and foster items or administrations that resound with individuals.

Vital Reasoning: Modern pioneers are key scholars who can see the master plan and set out to arrive at their associations. They can offset transient targets with long haul objectives and plan appropriately.

Relational abilities: Having the option to impart their vision and thoughts obviously is a sign of modern pioneers. They rouse and inspire their groups and partners with their words and activities.

Moral Authority: Uprightness and moral way of behaving are non-debatable for modern pioneers. They set an ethical compass for their associations and show others how its done in issues of morals and social obligation.

Impact and Effect: At long last, modern pioneers affect their enterprises, social orders, and, surprisingly, the world in general. They leave an enduring heritage and shape the course of history in their separate spaces.

All through this investigation, we will experience these traits and qualities in the lives and activities of different modern pioneers, over a wide span of time. As we inspect their accounts, we will acquire experiences into how they saddled these characteristics to drive change and make history.

In the pages that follow, we will dive into the lives and traditions of chosen modern pioneers, each addressing an alternate time, industry, and set of difficulties. From the modern upheaval to the computerized age, from assembling to space investigation, these pioneers have formed the world in exceptional ways. We will investigate their commitments, the difficulties they confronted, and the getting through effect of their work.

One can't examine modern initiative without digging into the significant effect of the Modern Upset, a time of quick industrialization that started in the late eighteenth 100 years. During this period, the world saw a seismic shift from agrarian and handcraft-based economies to modern and assembling driven ones. This change was driven by a rush of mechanical developments, and at the very front of this change was James Watt.

James Watt was brought into the world dressed in Greenock, Scotland, in 1736, when the steam motor was in its earliest stages. He would proceed to become perhaps of the main figure in the improvement of steam power. Watt's commitments to steam motor innovation were instrumental in moving the Modern Unrest forward.

Watt's excursion into steam motor improvement started when he was approached to fix a model of Thomas Newcomen's steam motor in 1764. Newcomen's motor had been utilized for siphoning water out of mines, yet it was profoundly wasteful. Watt perceived the potential for development and set about planning a more productive variant.

The key development that put Watt's steam motor aside was the different condenser. By permitting the steam to be consolidated in a different chamber, he essentially diminished energy misfortune and extraordinarily worked on the motor's proficiency. This leap forward, licensed in 1769, denoted a defining moment throughout the entire existence of steam power.

Watt proceeded to refine and develop his plan, and he additionally collaborated with money manager Matthew Boulton to produce and sell his motors. This organization was a business accomplishment as well as a demonstration of Watt's capacity to team up and fabricate vital partnerships, a trademark frequently tracked down in modern pioneers.

The reception of Watt's steam motor achieved a sensational change in different ventures. It reformed assembling by giving a more solid and strong wellspring of mechanical power. Processing plants and factories across the Unified Realm and past immediately embraced Watt's motors, prompting expanded creation limit and more prominent industrialization.

1.1 Defining economic powerhouses

Monetary forces to be reckoned with are nations, districts, or substances that employ critical impact in the worldwide economy. These elements are described by their significant financial result, enormous populaces, high level foundation, and the capacity to shape global exchange and money. In this thorough investigation, we will dive into the variables that characterize monetary forces to be reckoned with, the authentic advancement of financial power, the ongoing central parts in the worldwide economy, and the likely future changes in financial power.

One of the essential factors that characterize financial forces to be reckoned with is their GDP (Gross domestic product). Gross domestic product estimates the all out financial result of a nation, and nations with higher GDPs commonly essentially affect the worldwide economy.

While Gross domestic product alone isn't the sole determinant of financial power, it is a critical sign of a country's generally monetary strength. Monetary forces to be reckoned with will generally have reliably high GDPs, which can be credited to a blend of variables, including a vigorous assembling area, a flourishing administrations industry, and a solid farming base.

Populace size is one more essential part of monetary power. Nations with enormous populaces frequently approach a huge workforce and purchaser market. This segment advantage permits them to deliver labor and products at scale, draw in unfamiliar speculation, and impact worldwide buyer patterns. For example, China and India, with their gigantic populaces, have become monetary goliaths due to a limited extent to their capacity to take advantage of their workforce and buyer base.

Foundation improvement assumes a huge part in the ascent of monetary forces to be reckoned with. An advanced framework, including transportation organizations, correspondence frameworks, and energy creation, is fundamental for working with monetary development. Financial forces to be reckoned with put vigorously in framework, which empowers them to productively move merchandise and individuals, associate with worldwide business sectors, and cultivate development. This foundation benefit can give monetary forces to be reckoned with an upper hand in global exchange and financial turn of events.

Monetary broadening is a vital quality of financial forces to be reckoned with. These substances frequently have assorted economies with numerous areas adding to their Gross domestic product. This enhancement gives solidness and strength, as it lessens dependence on a solitary industry or area. For instance, the US, one of the world's driving financial forces to be reckoned with, has a differentiated economy with commitments from areas like innovation, medical services, money, and assembling.

Development and mechanical progression are significant drivers of monetary power. Nations and districts that put resources into innovative work, training, and innovation framework will more often than not have an upper hand in the worldwide economy. Development not just prompts the making of new items and ventures yet in addition builds efficiency and productivity. Mechanical ability can give financial forces to be reckoned with an edge in worldwide rivalry, as it empowers them to remain at the very front of arising ventures.

Political security and a favorable business climate are fundamental for monetary forces to be reckoned with to flourish. Financial backers and organizations are bound to work in nations with stable legislatures, straightforward guidelines, and solid property privileges assurance. These variables add to a good business environment that draws in venture and advances monetary development. Nations like Switzerland and Singapore are known for their political solidness and business-accommodating conditions, which have added to their status as monetary forces to be reckoned with.

Exchange and worldwide coordination assume a pivotal part in characterizing monetary forces to be reckoned with. Countries that participate in worldwide exchange, have a critical presence in worldwide stock chains, and are individuals from significant economic alliance will quite often have a more significant monetary impact. Exchange permits nations to get to new business sectors, import fundamental assets, and expand their monetary ties. Financial forces to be reckoned with are much of the time key part in the worldwide exchange field, impacting exchange approaches and molding global business.

Monetary strength is one more main attribute of financial forces to be reckoned with. An advanced monetary area, including strong banking and capital business sectors, is fundamental for working with ventures, capital stream, and financial strength. Monetary forces to be reckoned with commonly have complex monetary frameworks that draw in worldwide financial backers and permit them to productively assign assets. Monetary business sectors in New York, London, and Tokyo, for instance, are among the world's biggest and generally powerful.

Normal assets can be both a gift and a revile for monetary forces to be reckoned with. Nations plentiful in significant assets, like oil, minerals, or arable land, can become monetary forces to be reckoned with through asset trades. Be that as it may, dependence on these assets can likewise prompt financial weakness, as asset costs are in many cases subject to unpredictability. Monetary forces to be reckoned with that deal with their asset abundance shrewdly and differentiate their economies will generally support their status over the long haul.

Verifiable Development of Monetary Power

The idea of monetary forces to be reckoned with has developed since forever ago. In old times, city-states like Athens and Rome held monetary influence because of their essential areas, shipping lanes, and agrarian overflows. As history unfurled, realms rose and fell, each with its financial focuses. The Silk Street worked with exchange between the East and West, with districts along the course, like the Center East and Focal Asia, becoming monetary forces to be reckoned with of their time.

During the Medieval times, the development of strong exchanging urban areas like Venice and Genoa in Europe exhibited the monetary impact of metropolitan focuses. The Renaissance time saw the ascent of shipper republics, for example, the Dutch Republic, which became financial monsters because of their exchange predominance and developments finance.

The Modern Unrest, which started in the late eighteenth hundred years in England, denoted a critical defining moment in the development of financial forces to be reckoned with. The capacity to outfit steam power and efficiently manufacture products changed the financial scene. England, trailed by other Western European nations and the US, became modern forces to be reckoned with. The ascent of these countries was portrayed by quick urbanization, mechanical headways, and the extension of their worldwide impact.

The twentieth century saw the rise of superpowers, remarkably the US and the Soviet Association, during the Virus War. The two countries held colossal financial and military power, molding worldwide governmental issues and financial matters. The post-The Second Great War time frame saw the foundation of organizations like the Assembled Countries, Global Financial Asset (IMF), and World Bank, which intended to advance worldwide monetary dependability and participation.

The last 50% of the twentieth century additionally saw the financial ascent of Asian nations, like Japan and the "Four Asian Tigers" (South Korea, Taiwan, Hong Kong, and Singapore). These countries accomplished quick monetary development through industrialization and commodity drove advancement. China's financial changes, started in the last part of the 1970s, denoted a vital second in the worldwide monetary scene, as it changed into one of the world's financial forces to be reckoned with.

The present Major Monetary Forces to be reckoned with

In the 21st hundred years, a few nations and locales have arisen as major monetary forces to be reckoned with, each with its remarkable assets and difficulties. Coming up next are a portion of the conspicuous players in the worldwide economy:

US: The US stays a predominant financial force to be reckoned with the world's biggest Gross domestic product. Its economy is described by variety, with flourishing areas like innovation, medical care, money, and assembling. The U.S. likewise profits by an advanced foundation, a culture of development, and profound monetary business sectors.

China: China's monetary rising is one of the main accounts of the 21st 100 years. It flaunts the world's second-biggest Gross domestic product and a quickly developing working class. China has utilized its assembling capacities and product situated development methodology to turn into a worldwide financial power. It is additionally vigorously putting resources into innovation and advancement, with organizations like Alibaba and Tencent acquiring worldwide noticeable quality.

Japan: Japan, while confronting segment difficulties, stays an imposing financial force to be reckoned with. It has a profoundly trend setting innovation area, solid assembling base, and a culture of development. Japanese organizations like Toyota and Sony keep on driving in their particular businesses.

Germany: Germany is a monetary force to be reckoned with in Europe, known for its hearty assembling area, especially in the auto business. It benefits from a talented labor, serious areas of strength for force direction, and a promise to innovative work.

India: With its huge and energetic populace, India is ready to turn into a significant monetary force to be reckoned with in the next few decades. It has a developing administrations area, including data innovation and business process reevaluating, and is making progress in assembling and framework improvement.

Russia: Russia, with its tremendous normal assets, is a monetary force to be reckoned with in the energy area. Its energy trades, including oil and gaseous petrol, give it critical impact in worldwide energy markets. In any case, Russia faces financial difficulties because of worldwide authorizations and political unsteadiness.

Brazil: Brazil, as one of the BRICS nations, is a significant monetary force to be reckoned with in South America. It is known for its horticultural and mining enterprises, yet it likewise faces financial difficulties connected with imbalance and political shakiness.

South Korea: South Korea's fast industrialization and mechanical headways have made it a worldwide monetary force to be reckoned with. Organizations like Samsung and Hyundai are universally perceived, and the country.

1.2 The significance of industrial leaders in the global economy

Modern pioneers assume a vital part in molding the worldwide economy. These are nations or districts with exceptionally created modern areas, high level assembling capacities, and a solid presence in worldwide exchange. In this thorough investigation, we will dig into the meaning of modern pioneers, the authentic development of industrialization, the ongoing central parts in the worldwide modern scene, and the effect of these pioneers on different parts of the worldwide economy.

The meaning of modern forerunners in the worldwide economy can be perceived from different perspectives, every one of which adds to their crucial job in forming the monetary scene. These modern chiefs are portrayed by a few key credits, which incorporate cutting edge innovation, elevated degrees of development, solid work markets, admittance to capital, and vigorous framework. These traits aggregately cultivate a climate helpful for industrialization, empowering them to lead in the worldwide economy.

Cutting edge innovation is a foundation of modern initiative. Modern pioneers put vigorously in innovative work, bringing about state of the art advances, which, thusly, drive development and efficiency gains. These progressions empower the creation of greater products, further developed proficiency, and frequently, the advancement of altogether new businesses. For example, pioneers in the tech area, like the US and South Korea, have spearheaded developments in semiconductors, broadcast communications, and customer gadgets.

Development is one more sign of modern pioneers. These nations and districts have a culture that empowers inventiveness and business, prompting the introduction of new ventures and the persistent improvement of existing ones. Through development, they stay serious in the worldwide commercial center as well as started precedents and principles that shape the direction of worldwide ventures.

Solid work markets add to the meaning of modern pioneers. These pioneers gloat gifted and useful labor forces that are equipped for executing mind boggling undertakings and adding to great creation. Much of the time, their work markets are prepared to adjust to evolving requests, making them strong to shifts in innovation and market patterns.

Admittance to capital is fundamental for supporting modern authority. Modern pioneers frequently have created monetary areas that can effectively dispense cash-flow to useful undertakings. Admittance to funding, advances, and value markets permits organizations to put resources into exploration, improvement, and development, cultivating modern development and intensity.

Hearty framework is another key trait. Modern pioneers have advanced transportation organizations, energy frameworks, and correspondence foundation, empowering the proficient development of merchandise, the stock of energy, and worldwide network. Framework speculation adds to both homegrown and worldwide seriousness.

Authentic Advancement of Industrialization

The authentic advancement of industrialization gives setting to grasping the meaning of modern forerunners in the worldwide economy. Industrialization is an interaction that traverses hundreds of years, with every time set apart by its interesting achievements and effects on the worldwide monetary scene.

The Main Modern Upheaval, which started in the late eighteenth hundred years in England, presented motorization and the utilization of steam power. It prompted the development of material assembling, the improvement of the processing plant framework, and a shift from agrarian social orders to modern ones. The Unified Realm arose as the main modern pioneer, molding the course of current industrialization.

The Second Modern Transformation, which happened in the late nineteenth and mid twentieth hundreds of years, saw the broad reception of power and the gas powered motor. This time achieved huge headways in transportation, correspondence, and modern cycles. The US, with its huge regular assets, turned into a noticeable modern pioneer, especially in areas like steel, car assembling, and synthetic substances.

The Third Modern Upheaval, frequently connected with the mid-twentieth hundred years, presented gadgets, PCs, and mechanization. This time saw the ascent of Japan and Germany as modern pioneers, with their assets in auto assembling and hardware. The effect of the Third Modern Unrest broadened all around the world, as these innovations worked with global exchange and network.

The Fourth Modern Unrest, which started in the late twentieth hundred years and go on today, is described by the digitalization of different businesses, the web, and the assembly of advances like computerized reasoning and biotechnology.

The US, as a tech force to be reckoned with, has driven in this period, with organizations like Apple, Google, and Amazon reshaping worldwide businesses and shopper conduct.

The Ongoing Major Modern Pioneers

In the 21st 100 years, a few nations and locales stand apart as major modern pioneers, each contributing essentially to the worldwide economy. These modern chiefs keep on forming businesses and impact global exchange. Coming up next are a portion of the unmistakable players in the worldwide modern scene:

US: The US stays a worldwide modern pioneer, especially in innovation, aviation, car, and drugs. Silicon Valley is an image of development, and organizations like Tesla, Boeing, and Pfizer have a significant worldwide impression. The U.S. likewise keeps areas of strength for an in the energy area, with progressions in shale gas and environmentally friendly power advancements.

China: China's quick industrialization and assembling capacities have made it a worldwide modern force to be reckoned with. The nation leads in different areas, including hardware, media communications, and steel creation. It has utilized its assembling ability to turn into the world's processing plant, creating merchandise for both home-grown and global business sectors.

Germany: Known for its accuracy designing and car fabricating, Germany is a critical modern forerunner in Europe. The nation is home to eminent organizations like Volkswagen, Siemens, and Bosch. It is likewise a forerunner in the sustainable power area, with a solid spotlight on clean innovations.

Japan: Japan stays a forerunner in hardware, auto assembling, and accuracy apparatus. Organizations like Toyota, Sony, and Panasonic keep on setting worldwide norms in their particular businesses. Japan's attention on quality and development guarantees its proceeded with importance in the worldwide modern scene.

South Korea: South Korea's modern ability is apparent in areas like semiconductors, shopper gadgets, and shipbuilding. Organizations like Samsung, LG, and Hyundai have accomplished global acknowledgment. South Korea's commitment to innovative work has permitted it to keep up with its situation as a significant modern player.

Taiwan: Taiwan is known for its semiconductor producing, with organizations like TSMC (Taiwan Semiconductor Assembling Organization) being basic to the worldwide tech store network. The country's aptitude in chip creation and hardware plays set its part as a modern chief.

Switzerland: Switzerland is a forerunner in accuracy instruments, drugs, and monetary administrations. Swiss organizations like Novartis and Roche are critical players in the drug business, while the nation's financial area is known for its security and worldwide reach.

India: India's modern authority is developing, especially in the data innovation and programming administrations area. The country's IT organizations, including Goodbye Consultancy Administrations (TCS) and Infosys, offer types of assistance to clients around the world. India's product and innovation abilities have added to its financial importance.

Canada: Canada is a modern forerunner in regular asset businesses, including energy, mining, and ranger service. The country's bountiful normal assets and solid mining and energy areas add to its part in worldwide industry.

Singapore: Singapore is a significant modern forerunner in Southeast Asia, with an emphasis on hardware, aviation, and biotechnology. The country's essential area and business-accommodating climate have drawn in worldwide organizations and cultivated modern development.

Influence on the Worldwide Economy

Modern pioneers significantly affect different parts of the worldwide economy. Their importance reaches out to worldwide exchange, mechanical development, business, supply chains, and generally monetary dependability.

Global Exchange: Modern pioneers are key part in worldwide exchange, as they produce and product a huge piece of the world's labor and products. Their exchange exercises impact worldwide stockpile chains, and their imports frequently drive the financial fortunes of different countries. The volume of exchange they participate in can likewise influence worldwide exchange approaches and arrangements.

Mechanical Development: These pioneers are at the front line of mechanical progressions, frequently driving advancement in their separate ventures. Their innovative work endeavors bring about the making of new items, administrations, and cycles that benefit the worldwide economy. Moreover, their advancements can prompt the improvement of completely new ventures, setting out open doors for financial development and work.

Work: Modern pioneers regularly areas of strength for have markets, giving business amazing open doors to a great many individuals. The presence of these pioneers can make occupations both straightforwardly and in a roundabout way, as their exercises support different areas, including providers, coordinated factors, and administrations. Work creation adds to generally financial prosperity and soundness.

1.3 Overview of the countries to be discussed

In this complete investigation, we will dive into a choice of nations from various districts of the world, each with its extraordinary qualities, history, culture, and financial importance. These nations play played significant parts in molding their separate areas and the worldwide scene. They address a different exhibit of societies, political frameworks, financial designs, and verifiable foundations, offering a rich embroidery of experiences into the intricacies of our globalized world.

US:

The US, frequently alluded to as the USA, is an immense and various nation situated in North America. With a populace of north of 330 million individuals, it is the world's third-most crowded country. The US is a government republic involving 50 states and a capital locale, Washington, D.C. It is known for its rich history, various culture, and a solid obligation to a majority rules government and individual opportunities.

Financially, the US is the world's biggest economy, described by an exceptionally evolved modern and administration area. It is home to various worldwide organizations, mechanical trend-setters, and a unique monetary market focused in Money Road. Its monetary impact stretches out across the globe, making it a vital participant in worldwide exchange, speculation, and monetary dependability.

The country's political framework is described by a vote based type of government with a detachment of abilities between the chief, regulative, and legal branches. The US has been a noticeable player in foreign relations, with a huge effect on worldwide legislative issues, security, and discretion.

China:

China, formally known as Individuals' Republic of China, is a huge country in East Asia with a populace of over 1.4 billion individuals, making it the world's most crowded country. China is known for its rich history, culture, and civilization, going back millennia. It hosts a solitary gathering communist arrangement of government drove by the Chinese Socialist Faction (CCP).

Monetarily, China has gone through a surprising change throughout the course of recent many years. It has developed from a transcendently agrarian culture into the world's second-biggest economy. China's financial development has been portrayed by fast industrialization, urbanization, and product situated improvement. It has areas of strength for an area and is a worldwide forerunner in the creation of merchandise going from gadgets to materials.

China's job in worldwide exchange, international strategy, and worldwide stock chains is principal. It has turned into a central part in the worldwide economy, with huge impact in global associations and economic accords. The country's accentuation on development and innovative headway has prompted the ascent of compelling tech organizations like Huawei, Alibaba, and Tencent.

Germany:

Germany, situated in Focal Europe, is known for its rich history, culture, and commitments to science, reasoning, and artistic expression. It is a government parliamentary republic and the biggest economy in Europe. Germany is perceived for its designing ability, accuracy fabricating, and an advanced government assistance state.

Financially, Germany is a modern chief, with a solid accentuation on cutting edge producing, especially in the auto area. Organizations like Volkswagen, BMW, and Mercedes-Benz are inseparable from German designing and development. Germany's solid monetary area, remembering its stock trade for Frankfurt, assumes a huge part in Europe's monetary scene.

Germany's political framework is described by a parliamentary majority rules system, with a solid obligation to natural manageability and social government assistance. The nation's impact in the European Association (EU) has been significant, making it a central member in molding European strategies and guidelines.

India:

India, situated in South Asia, is the world's second-most crowded country, with over 1.3 billion individuals. It is known for its antiquated history, various culture, and huge commitments to math, reasoning, and artistic expression. India works as a government parliamentary popularity based republic.

Monetarily, India is a rising worldwide financial force to be reckoned with. It has a different economy with qualities in data innovation, programming administrations, drugs, horticulture, and assembling. India's IT industry, with organizations like Goodbye Consultancy Administrations (TCS) and Infosys, serves clients around the world. The country's dynamic business venture and developing working class have added to its financial importance.

India's political scene is set apart by a multi-party a majority rule government, and it is quite possibly of the biggest vote based system on the planet. Its job in worldwide undertakings has been developing, and it is an individual from different global associations, including the Unified Countries and the World Exchange Association.

Brazil:

Brazil, the biggest country in South America, is known for its assorted culture, tremendous rainforests, and dynamic Amusement park festivities. It works as a government official republic and is the world's fifth-most crowded country.

Financially, Brazil is a modern forerunner in South America, with qualities in farming, mining, and energy creation. It is a significant exporter of rural items, including soybeans, espresso, and hamburger. Brazil additionally has critical oil saves, and its energy area has added to its financial significance in the locale.

Brazil's political framework is portrayed by an official majority rules government. The nation plays had a critical impact in local discretion and is an individual from associations like the Association of South American Countries (UNASUR) and the Local area of Latin American and Caribbean States (CELAC).

Japan:

Japan, an island country in East Asia, has a rich history, culture, and custom. It works as an established government with a parliamentary government. Japan is known for its mechanical development, restrained hard working attitude, and commitments to the fields of gadgets, advanced mechanics, and transportation.

Financially, Japan is a modern chief with qualities in car producing, purchaser gadgets, and accuracy hardware. Organizations like Toyota, Sony, and Panasonic have a worldwide presence. Japan's obligation to innovative work has permitted it to keep up with its situation as a significant modern player.

Japan's political framework is described by a parliamentary majority rule government. The nation plays had a huge impact in territorial security, exchange, and strategy, and it is an individual from worldwide associations like the Unified Countries and the Gathering of Seven (G7).

Russia:

Russia, the biggest country on the planet, ranges Eastern Europe and northern Asia. It works as a government semi-official republic. Russia has a celebrated history, with a huge effect on world writing, craftsmanship, and legislative issues.

Financially, Russia is a modern forerunner in energy creation, especially in oil and petroleum gas. It is a significant exporter of energy assets and essentially affects worldwide energy markets. In any case, Russia likewise faces financial difficulties, including worldwide authorizations and political flimsiness.

Russia's political framework is portrayed by a semi-official vote based system, however it has confronted analysis with respect to political opportunities and common freedoms. It is an individual from associations like the Unified Countries and the Shanghai Participation Association (SCO).

South Korea:

South Korea, situated on the Korean Promontory, is known for its quick industrialization, mechanical advancement, and financial development. It works as a popularity based republic. South Korea has made huge commitments to mainstream society, including K-popular music and Korean film.

Monetarily, South Korea is a modern chief, especially in the creation of semiconductors, purchaser gadgets, and shipbuilding. Organizations like Samsung, LG, and Hyundai have accomplished global acknowledgment. South Korea's accentuation on innovative work has permitted it to keep up with its situation as a significant modern player.

South Korea's political framework is described by an official majority rules government. The nation plays had a huge impact in local security and tact and is an individual from associations like the Unified Countries and the Association for Financial Collaboration and Improvement (OECD).

Chapter 2

The United States: A Tradition of Economic Supremacy

The US has a well established custom of monetary matchless quality that has formed the country's personality and impacted the worldwide financial scene. This custom is established in authentic, political, and financial variables that have impelled the US to its ongoing situation as one of the world's driving monetary powers.

One of the key factors that added to the US's monetary matchless quality is its set of experiences of business venture and advancement. Over now is the ideal time, the US has been a hotbed of pioneering movement, with people and organizations continually pushing the limits of what is conceivable. From the beginning of toward the west development and the gold rush to the tech blast of the twentieth and 21st hundreds of years, American business visionaries have been at the front line of monetary advancement. This soul of business venture has been a main impetus behind the country's financial achievement.

The US's obligation to an unrestricted economy has likewise assumed a huge part in its monetary matchless quality. The country's organizers had faith in the significance of financial opportunity and restricted government mediation in the economy. This way of thinking, cherished in the Constitution, has cultivated a business-accommodating climate that empowers rivalry, development, and venture. The US has a strong lawful and administrative structure that safeguards property privileges, upholds contracts, and guarantees a level battleground for organizations and people. This obligation to monetary opportunity has drawn in both homegrown and worldwide capital, prompting a dynamic and cutthroat commercial center.

One more significant part of the US's monetary matchless quality is its immense and different regular assets. The country's geographic size and shifted scene give an abundance of assets, from prolific farmland to bountiful mineral stores. The US has had the option to outfit these assets to fuel its monetary development, from the agrarian blast of the nineteenth 100 years to the energy insurgency of the twentieth 100 years. Admittance to such assets has permitted the country to keep major areas of strength for a strong economy, even in the midst of emergency.

Besides, the US has an advanced framework that works with financial development. The country's transportation organizations, including an immense street framework, ports, and air terminals, have been basic in empowering the development of merchandise and individuals. Moreover, the US has a profoundly evolved broadcast communications and web framework, which has been instrumental in the development of data innovation and online business ventures. This foundation has upheld the development of organizations and the productive dispersion of labor and products.

The US's arrangement of advanced education has likewise been a critical supporter of its financial incomparability. The nation brags an enormous number incredibly famous colleges and exploration foundations, which have created earth shattering examination and developments. American colleges have been at the cutting edge of mechanical headways, clinical forward leaps, and logical revelations. The accessibility of a profoundly gifted and taught labor force has drawn in worldwide ability and added to the country's mechanical and monetary initiative.

Notwithstanding these inside factors, the US's part in foreign relations has been vital in keeping up with its financial matchless quality. The country has been a defender of deregulation and a functioning member in global associations like the World Exchange Association (WTO). This obligation to worldwide exchange has permitted American organizations to grow their range and access new business sectors. It has likewise assisted with laying out the US as a worldwide monetary pioneer.

The US has likewise been instrumental in molding the global financial framework. The U.S. dollar fills in as the world's essential save cash, and numerous nations hold huge unfamiliar trade holds in dollars. This status gives the US impressive impact over worldwide monetary business sectors and permits it to back its shortages more effectively than different nations. The dependability and unwavering quality of the U.S. dollar have been vital in working with worldwide exchange and speculation.

The country's capacity to adjust to changing financial circumstances and difficulties has been one more key component of its monetary matchless quality. The US has endured various monetary emergencies, from the Economic crisis of the early 20s of the 1930s to the monetary emergency of 2008. For each situation, the nation has exhibited flexibility and versatility, executing arrangements and changes that have permitted it to recuperate and develop. This capacity to gain from previous slip-ups and develop has been a sign of the U.S. economy.

Besides, the US has major areas of strength for an of magnanimity and magnanimous giving. Large numbers of the most well off people and enterprises in the nation contribute critical sums to different causes and drives. This culture of giving has helped help schooling, medical services, and social projects, upgrading the general personal satisfaction and social dependability in the US. It has likewise added to the country's standing as a dependable and caring worldwide pioneer.

The US's practice of monetary matchless quality isn't without its difficulties and reactions. Pay imbalance has been a tenacious issue, with inconsistencies between the richest and the remainder of the populace. This issue has prompted banters about abundance rearrangement and the job of government in tending to imbalance. Moreover, ecological worries and the effect of industrialization have brought up issues about the maintainability of the country's monetary model. These moves require progressing consideration and activity to guarantee the proceeded with outcome of the U.S. economy.

The worldwide scene is continually developing, and the US faces rivalry from arising financial powers, like China and India. These countries have encountered quick monetary development and can possibly challenge the US's situation. The US should proceed to adjust and develop to keep up with its monetary administration in an impacting world.

As of late, there has been a developing spotlight on innovation and computerized advancement as drivers of monetary development. Silicon Valley in California has turned into a worldwide center point for innovation and development, with organizations like Apple, Google, and Facebook driving the way. The US's predominance in the tech area has been a huge consider its financial matchless quality, and it will probably keep on assuming a critical part in the country's future monetary achievement.

The US's practice of financial incomparability has not been without its reasonable portion of monetary emergencies. The Economic crisis of the early 20s of the 1930s was quite possibly of the most extreme monetary slump in the country's set of experiences. It brought about far and wide joblessness, neediness, and languishing. Notwithstanding, the U.S. government answered with the New Arrangement, a progression of changes and strategies pointed toward resuscitating the economy and giving social wellbeing nets to the American public. The New Arrangement included drives like the Non military personnel Protection Corps, which gave occupations to young fellows, and the Government managed retirement Act, which laid out an arrangement of retirement benefits. These projects settled the economy and established the groundwork for future financial development.

The monetary difficulties of the 1970s, including stagflation and the oil emergency, tried the versatility of the U.S. Once more economy. Notwithstanding, creative arrangements and strategies, like liberation and the advancement of unrestricted economy standards, added to a resurgence of financial development during the 1980s. The Reagan organization, specifically, supported a favorable to business plan, decreasing duties and advancing business venture. This approach lastingly affected the U.S. economy and is frequently connected with the period of Reaganomics.

The US confronted one more critical monetary emergency in 2008 with the worldwide monetary implosion. The real estate market bubble burst, prompting an extreme downturn and boundless monetary unsteadiness. Accordingly, the U.S. government ordered the Pained Resource Help Program (Canvas) and carried out a progression of measures to balance out the financial area and invigorate monetary recuperation. The Central bank likewise assumed a significant part by bringing down financing costs and carrying out quantitative facilitating. These endeavors assisted the country with rising up out of the emergency and return to a way of monetary development.

The continuous discussion about the job of government in the economy has been a focal subject in the US's practice of financial matchless quality.

The country's establishing standards underline restricted government mediation and the significance of individual freedom and property privileges. In any case, the degree to which government ought to control and support the economy has been a disputed matter over now is the right time.

On one side of the discussion are defenders of an additional hands-off approach, contending for insignificant unofficial law and lower charges. They accept that unregulated economy standards empower advancement, contest, and financial development. This viewpoint has frequently been related with moderate and freedom advocate belief systems, and it was especially compelling during the Reagan period.

On the opposite side of the discussion are advocates for a more dynamic government job in the economy. They contend that administration intercession is important to address market disappointments, safeguard shoppers, and guarantee social government assistance. This point of view has frequently been related with moderate and liberal philosophies and has prompted arrangements, for example, the New Arrangement and the foundation of social wellbeing nets like Federal retirement aide and Government health care.

2.1 Historical context of the U.S. as an industrial leader

The US's ascent as a modern chief can be followed back to its rich verifiable setting, enveloping a huge number of variables and critical minutes that have added to its financial predominance. From the beginning of European colonization to the present, the country's excursion to modern transcendence has been formed by advancement, monetary arrangements, geographic benefits, and cultural changes.

The pioneer time frame denoted the start of America's modern direction. The European pilgrims who showed up in the seventeenth century carried with them different abilities and advancements, which assumed a major part in molding the monetary scene representing things to come US. Horticulture was a focal concentration during this period, with harvests like tobacco, cotton, and indigo becoming significant money crops in the southern settlements. In the North, enterprises like shipbuilding and material assembling started to arise, making way for the country's modern turn of events.

The eighteenth century saw the development of a beginning modern area in America. This period was set apart by progressions in innovation and the multiplication of limited scope fabricating. The development of the cotton gin by Eli Whitney in 1793 reformed cotton creation, making it a significant driver of the Southern economy. Moreover, advancements in water-controlled apparatus and the expansion of early plants established the groundwork for industrialization.

The mid nineteenth century achieved critical monetary changes in the US. The Louisiana Buy in 1803 and the resulting toward the west development opened up huge terrains for settlement and horticulture.

The development of the Erie Channel during the 1820s worked with transportation and exchange, associating the Incomparable Lakes to the Atlantic Sea. These improvements set out new open doors for monetary development and assumed an essential part in the country's industrialization.

The rise of the material business in New Britain during the mid nineteenth century was a urgent crossroads in American modern history. The area's bountiful water assets and admittance to unrefined components, like cotton from the South, made it an optimal area for material creation. The utilization of force weavers turning machines upset the business, and New Britain became known as the "Material Belt." This early industrialization was a forerunner to the more extensive change that would happen in the next few decades.

One more basic advancement during this period was the extension of the transportation organization. The development of the principal U.S. rail lines, starting with the Baltimore and Ohio Railroad during the 1820s, upset the development of products and individuals. Rail lines made it conceivable to ship natural substances and completed items all the more proficiently, prodding monetary development and working with industrialization.

The mid-nineteenth century saw the combination of different elements that sped up industrialization in the US. The California Dash for unheard of wealth of 1848 pulled in an enormous convergence of individuals, adding to the country's populace development and encouraging an interest for labor and products. The disclosure of oil in Pennsylvania during the 1850s denoted the introduction of the U.S. petrol industry, further differentiating the country's modern base.

The Nationwide conflict, which seethed from 1861 to 1865, significantly affected American industrialization. The requests of the conflict exertion drove developments in assembling and transportation. Plants delivered weapons, ammo, and military gear on an extraordinary scale. The far reaching utilization of rail lines for troop and supply development featured the significance of this method of transportation. Following the conflict, the US was left with a powerful modern framework that could be bridled for peacetime monetary development.

The late nineteenth century is frequently alluded to as the "Plated Age," a time of fast industrialization and financial extension. Mechanical headways in steel creation, exemplified by the advancements of Andrew Carnegie and his Carnegie Steel Enterprise, changed the development business and laid the preparation for the cutting edge high rise. The improvement of the Bessemer cycle, which took into consideration the large scale manufacturing of steel, made it a foundation of American industry.

The coming of the cross-country railroad in 1869, which associated the East Coast toward the West Coast, was a pivotal accomplishment in transportation foundation. It worked with the development of individuals, products, and assets the nation over, opening up new business sectors and valuable open doors for organizations.

This extension of rail lines, joined with the consummation of the Principal Cross-country Railroad, significantly affected financial development and assumed a pivotal part in the country's modern domination.

The late nineteenth century likewise saw the rise of large companies and modern titans. Business visionaries like John D. Rockefeller (Standard Oil), J.P. Morgan (banking and money), and Cornelius Vanderbilt (railways) assumed vital parts in solidifying ventures and building strong business realms. While their union of force raised worries about imposing business models and trusts, it additionally drove mechanical advancement and expanded effectiveness in different areas of the economy.

The time was set apart by a flood in mechanical developments. Thomas Edison's advancement of the electric light and the foundation of General electric homes and organizations, improving efficiency and changing daily existence. The phone, concocted by Alexander Graham Ringer, changed correspondence, while the improvement of the phonograph and films laid the basis for media outlets.

The mid twentieth century was a time of proceeded with modern extension and development. The development of the auto business, with pioneers like Henry Portage and the presentation of the sequential construction system, changed transportation and assembling. Large scale manufacturing procedures considered the proficient and financially savvy creation of purchaser merchandise, making them more open to a more extensive area of the populace.

The Second Great War, which occurred from 1914 to 1918, altogether affected the U.S. economy. The conflict exertion drove interest for American merchandise and materials, further helping modern creation. After the conflict, the US encountered a time of financial development known as the "Thundering Twenties," described by industrialism, monetary success, and the rise of new businesses.

The securities exchange crash of 1929 denoted the start of the Economic crisis of the early 20s, quite possibly of the most difficult financial period in American history. The Downturn was portrayed by far reaching joblessness, business disappointments, and financial difficulty. The U.S. government carried out different projects and arrangements under President Franklin D. Roosevelt's New Arrangement to address the monetary emergency, including framework advancement, work creation, and monetary area guideline.

The Second Great War, which happened from 1939 to 1945, significantly affected the US's modern limit. The nation moved into a conflict economy, with enterprises prepared for the creation of weapons, vehicles, and supplies. This wartime exertion not just assumed a vital part in the loss of the Pivot drives yet in addition kicked off the American economy, making a large number of occupations and invigorating modern development.

After The Second Great War, the US encountered a time of phenomenal financial thriving. The GI Bill, passed in 1944, gave instructive and lodging advantages to veterans, empowering them to seek after advanced education and homeownership. The development of rural lodging improvements and the development of the auto business filled suburbanization and financial development.

The post-war time likewise saw the ascent of the US as a worldwide financial superpower. The country's modern limit and financial strength made it a prevailing player in the global monetary scene. The Bretton Woods Meeting in 1944 laid out another global financial framework, with the U.S. dollar as the world's essential save money. The US likewise assumed a vital part in the foundation of the Global Financial Asset (IMF) and the World Bank, forming the structure of global money.

2.2 Factors contributing to the United States' economic strength

The US has reliably kept a place of financial strength and initiative on the worldwide stage. This getting through status is the consequence of a complicated exchange of various variables that have added to the country's monetary matchless quality. Analyzing these variables, from verifiable roots to contemporary conditions, is crucial for grasping the country's monetary ability.

One of the critical variables that have added to the US's monetary strength is its set of experiences of pioneering soul and development. From its initial days as a youngster country to its current status as a monetary force to be reckoned with, the US has been a favorable place for pioneering tries. This soul of development and chance taking has impelled the country to the bleeding edge of innovative headways and monetary leap forwards. Models flourish, from the early trailblazers who wandered toward the west during the Gold Rush to the tech business people of the 21st century who have changed ventures through momentous advancements.

The obligation to an unregulated economy is one more basic component of the US's financial strength. This philosophy is profoundly imbued in the country's personality, coming from its establishing standards. The U.S. Constitution, which lays out the structure for the country's monetary and political establishments, advances the possibility of financial opportunity with restricted government mediation. This approach has established a business-accommodating climate that cultivates contest, empowers development, and draws in venture. The U.S. legitimate and administrative system further builds up this monetary opportunity, safeguarding property freedoms, implementing contracts, and guaranteeing a level battleground for organizations and people. This obligation to financial freedom has been a huge figure the US's monetary initiative.

The US's regular benefits, including its immense and various assets, have likewise assumed a critical part in its monetary strength. The country's tremendous geographic size and fluctuated scene offer an abundance of assets, from prolific farmland to plentiful mineral stores.

The capacity to outfit these assets has been instrumental in filling monetary development. From the rural blast of the nineteenth 100 years to the energy upheaval of the twentieth hundred years, the US has utilized its normal resources for keep serious areas of strength for a strong economy, even notwithstanding worldwide monetary difficulties.

Moreover, the US flaunts an advanced framework that improves financial development. The country's broad transportation organizations, including a broad street framework, ports, and air terminals, work with the development of products and individuals, both locally and globally. A profoundly evolved broadcast communications and web foundation play had a vital impact in cultivating the development of data innovation and web based business enterprises. This powerful foundation upholds the development of organizations and the effective conveyance of labor and products, adding to the country's monetary incomparability.

The US's arrangement of advanced education has been a foundation of its financial strength. The nation is home to a plenty of incredibly famous colleges and exploration foundations, which have reliably created pivotal examination and developments. American colleges have driven the way in mechanical headways, clinical leap forwards, and logical revelations. This accessibility of exceptionally gifted and taught ability has drawn in worldwide ability, further supporting the country's mechanical and monetary authority.

The US's job in foreign relations has additionally been instrumental in its monetary strength. The nation has reliably upheld with the expectation of complimentary exchange and has effectively taken part in global associations like the World Exchange Association (WTO). This obligation to worldwide exchange has worked with the development of American organizations, giving admittance to new business sectors and adding to the country's financial incomparability. The US's dynamic job in forming the worldwide financial framework is especially critical. The U.S. dollar fills in as the world's essential save cash, and numerous nations hold huge unfamiliar trade saves in dollars. This status concedes the US extensive impact over worldwide monetary business sectors and makes it simpler for the country to back its shortfalls contrasted with different countries. The soundness and reliability of the U.S. dollar play had a significant impact in the worldwide help of global exchange and speculation.

2.3 The role of innovation and technology

The job of development and innovation has been a foundation of the US's financial strength and administration in the worldwide field. Over now is the right time, the country has reliably embraced and driven mechanical progressions, encouraging a climate where development flourishes and assumes a vital part in the country's financial achievement shent. Analyzing the effect and meaning of development and innovation in the US is significant for figuring out its proceeded with financial matchless quality.

Advancement is well established in the American soul, tracing all the way back to the country's establishing. The early European pilgrims carried with them different abilities and advancements that assumed a critical part in forming the monetary scene representing things to come US.

As the country extended toward the west, trailblazers and designers added to the advancement of new instruments, hardware, and cycles that filled financial development. This soul of development has stayed a central quality of American culture, pushing the limits of what is conceivable.

Quite possibly of the most groundbreaking advancement in American history was the improvement of the cotton gin by Eli Whitney in 1793. This innovation changed cotton creation, making it one of the South's most critical money crops and a main impetus behind the locale's economy. The cotton gin's capacity to isolate cotton strands from seeds at a lot quicker rate than difficult work emphatically expanded cotton creation and benefit.

The mid nineteenth century saw the multiplication of water-controlled apparatus and the development of limited scope fabricating. Production lines started to jump up, adding to the beginning phases of industrialization. This period saw the most important moves toward what might later turn into an undeniable modern upset.

The mid-nineteenth century denoted one more basic stage in American development, driven by mechanical progressions and monetary open doors. The California Dash for unheard of wealth of 1848 baited masses of individuals toward the West Coast, helping the nation's populace and spurring an interest for labor and products. The disclosure of oil in Pennsylvania during the 1850s denoted the start of the U.S. petrol industry, expanding the country's modern base and giving a huge energy asset.

The Nationwide conflict, which seethed from 1861 to 1865, significantly affected American development and innovation. The requests of the conflict exertion drove advancements in assembling and transportation. Processing plants efficiently manufactured weapons, ammo, and military hardware, featuring the capability of large scale manufacturing and sequential construction system techniques. The inescapable utilization of railways for troop and supply developments highlighted the significance of this method of transportation. Following the conflict, the US was left with a vigorous modern framework that would be outfit for peacetime monetary development.

The late nineteenth 100 years, frequently alluded to as the "Overlaid Age," was set apart by fast industrialization and mechanical advances. Steel creation, exemplified by Andrew Carnegie and his Carnegie Steel Enterprise, changed the development business and established the groundwork for the cutting edge high rise. The improvement of the Bessemer cycle, which took into consideration the large scale manufacturing of steel, made it a foundation of American industry.

The improvement of the cross-country railroad in 1869, associating the East Coast toward the West Coast, was a great accomplishment in transportation framework. It worked with the development of products, individuals, and assets the country over, opening up new business sectors and valuable open doors for organizations.

This extension of rail lines, combined with the fruition of the Primary Cross-country Railroad, significantly affected financial development, assuming a basic part in the country's modern domination.

The late nineteenth century likewise saw the ascent of large companies and modern titans. Business visionaries like John D. Rockefeller (Standard Oil), J.P. Morgan (banking and money), and Cornelius Vanderbilt (railways) assumed urgent parts in merging ventures and building strong business domains. While their union of force raised worries about syndications and trusts, it likewise drove mechanical advancement and expanded proficiency in different areas of the economy.

One of the characterizing highlights of the late nineteenth and mid twentieth hundreds of years was a flood in mechanical developments. Thomas Edison's improvement of the electric light and the foundation of General electric homes and organizations, upgrading efficiency and changing daily existence. The phone, concocted by Alexander Graham Ringer, altered correspondence, interfacing individuals across huge distances. Also, the improvement of the phonograph and movies laid the foundation for media outlets.

The mid twentieth century proceeded with the pattern of development and mechanical advancement, most remarkably with the rise of the car business. Trend-setters like Henry Passage and the presentation of the sequential construction system upset transportation and assembling. Large scale manufacturing strategies considered the proficient and savvy creation of customer products, making them more open to a more extensive area of the populace.

The Second Great War, which occurred from 1914 to 1918, altogether affected the U.S. economy and mechanical advancement. The conflict exertion drove interest for American merchandise and materials, further supporting modern creation. Following the conflict, the US encountered a time of monetary development known as the "Thundering Twenties," portrayed by industrialism, financial thriving, and the rise of new businesses.

The financial exchange crash of 1929 denoted the start of the Economic crisis of the early 20s, perhaps of the most difficult monetary period in American history. The Downturn was portrayed by broad joblessness, business disappointments, and financial difficulty. The U.S. government carried out different projects and approaches under President Franklin D. Roosevelt's New Arrangement to address the monetary emergency, including framework advancement, work creation, and monetary area guideline.

The Second Great War, which happened from 1939 to 1945, significantly affected the US's mechanical advancement and modern limit. The nation moved into a conflict economy, with businesses prepared for the development of weapons, vehicles, and supplies. This wartime exertion not just assumed a critical part in the loss of the Hub controls yet in addition kicked off the American economy, making a great many positions and invigorating modern development.

After The Second Great War, the US encountered a time of phenomenal financial thriving. The GI Bill, passed in 1944, gave instructive and lodging advantages to veterans, empowering them to seek after advanced education and homeownership. The development of rural lodging improvements and the development of the car business filled suburbanization and monetary development.

The post-war time likewise saw the ascent of the US as a worldwide financial superpower. The country's modern limit and monetary strength made it a prevailing player in the worldwide financial scene. The Bretton Woods Gathering in 1944 laid out another worldwide money related framework, with the U.S. dollar as the world's essential hold cash. The US assumed a urgent part in the foundation of the Global Financial Asset (IMF) and the World Bank, forming the system of worldwide money.

The 1950s and 1960s were set apart by the development of buyer culture and the rise of new innovations. The approach of TV changed diversion and correspondence, while the improvement of the space business and the send off of NASA's Apollo program denoted another outskirts for mechanical development. All the while, the advancement of the coordinated circuit, which prompted the formation of the microchip, was instrumental in the development of the innovation area and the possible ascent of the PC business.

The 1970s and 1980s brought the PC transformation, with organizations like Apple and Microsoft driving the way. The presentation of the IBM PC in 1981 denoted a huge second in the democratization of registering innovation. PCs turned out to be more available to the overall population, making way for the advanced age.

The late twentieth hundred years and mid 21st century have seen a computerized upheaval that has reshaped enterprises and changed the manner in which individuals live and work. The improvement of the web and the expansion of individualized computing gadgets, for example, cell phones and tablets, have set out new monetary open doors and disturbed customary plans of action. Organizations like Apple,

Amazon, and research have become worldwide goliaths, reshaping trade and correspondence. The US has been at the bleeding edge of this computerized change, with Silicon Valley in California filling in as a worldwide center point for innovation and development.

Lately, the US has confronted new mechanical difficulties and amazing open doors. The ascent of man-made consciousness (artificial intelligence), AI, and mechanization has brought up issues about the fate of work and business. These advancements can possibly build efficiency and productivity yet in addition present difficulties connected with work dislodging and labor force retraining. The US should explore these progressions to guarantee that its labor force stays versatile and cutthroat in a quickly developing mechanical scene.

The Coronavirus pandemic, which started in late 2019, significantly affected the job of innovation in the US's economy. The pandemic sped up the reception of advanced innovations and remote work, changing how organizations work and convey administrations. Web based business and online administrations experienced critical development, and the turn of events .

3

Chapter 3

China: The Rise of an Economic Giant

China's surprising rising as a monetary goliath is one of the main improvements of the 21st hundred years. The country's change from an agrarian culture into the world's second-biggest economy has been completely astounding. China's ascent has reshaped the worldwide financial scene as well as produced significant interest and discussion about the elements driving its monetary development and the ramifications of its recently discovered monetary power.

Verifiable Foundation

To comprehend China's monetary excursion, taking into account its authentic context is fundamental. The country's set of experiences is set apart by a rich embroidery of lines, domains, and times of both political strength and disturbance. Notwithstanding, it was during the twentieth century that China went through a groundbreaking occasion that would show it the way to financial noticeable quality: the Chinese Socialist Transformation.

In 1949, under the authority of Mao Zedong, the Chinese Socialist Faction laid out Individuals' Republic of China (PRC). This noticeable a critical takeoff from China's past political and financial frameworks.

The Socialist Coalition left on a progression of aggressive missions to reshape the nation's social, monetary, and political scene.

One of the most remarkable drives during this period was the Incomparable Jump Forward, sent off in the last part of the 1950s. The mission planned to industrialize and collectivize China's farming quickly. Be that as it may, it prompted far and wide starvation, financial difficulties, and social commotion, bringing about the passings of millions of individuals. This period exhibited the massive difficulties and intricacies of dealing with a nation of China's size and populace.

The Social Transformation, which occurred during the 1960s and 1970s, further upset China's social and monetary texture. It was a time of serious political and philosophical disturbance, prompting far and wide cleanses, oppression, and the concealment of scholarly and social articulation. The disturbance and stagnation during this time significantly affected the nation's turn of events.

China's Monetary Changes

The defining moment for China's monetary change came in the last part of the 1970s with the authority of Deng Xiaoping. Deng started a progression of monetary changes that moved China's financial strategies toward a more market-situated approach. This undeniable the start of the "change and opening-up" period, which significantly affected the country's monetary direction.

One of the main changes was the presentation of the Family Obligation Framework in farming. Under this framework, ranchers were allowed more independence and motivators to increment horticultural efficiency. This shift away from aggregate cultivating prompted expanded farming result and worked on expectations for everyday comforts in country regions.

China likewise started to open its economy to unfamiliar venture and exchange. Exceptional Monetary Zones (SEZs) were laid out in assigned regions to draw in unfamiliar venture and advance products. These zones gave impetuses and loosened up guidelines to urge global organizations to set up tasks in China.

The blend of market-situated changes, rural efficiency enhancements, and opening up to unfamiliar speculation and exchange made an establishment for China's financial development. The country's Gross domestic product started to extend at an exceptional speed, and it turned into a center point for worldwide assembling and commodity.

China's Monetary Triumphs

A few key elements have added to China's monetary victories and its development as a financial monster:

Assembling and Commodities: China's assembling area, described by low work costs and an immense labor force, turned into a worldwide creation center point. The country's capacity to create a large number of products at serious costs made it the "world's plant." Chinese commodities overwhelmed global business sectors, bringing about an exchange excess and significant unfamiliar trade saves.

Unfamiliar Direct Venture (FDI): China effectively pulled in unfamiliar speculation through its SEZs and different impetuses. Unfamiliar organizations looked to exploit China's developing shopper market and low creation costs. This flood of FDI brought innovation, skill, and cash-flow to the nation, adding to its modern turn of events.

Foundation Advancement: China put vigorously in framework, assembling a broad organization of streets, railroads, ports, and air terminals. This framework advancement worked on homegrown availability, diminished transportation costs, and worked with exchange.

Urbanization: The nation encountered an enormous rush of urbanization as individuals relocated from country regions to urban areas looking for better monetary open doors. The development of megacities like Beijing, Shanghai, and Shenzhen became images of China's urbanization pattern. This shift from agrarian to metropolitan living prompted expanded work efficiency and more noteworthy customer interest.

Training and Labor force: China focused on schooling and put resources into its labor force. The nation has a huge pool of profoundly talented specialists, designers, and researchers. Its accentuation on instruction and professional preparation has created a workforce equipped for driving mechanical headways and development.

State-Drove Free enterprise: China embraced an interesting monetary model frequently alluded to as "state-drove private enterprise." Under this model, the state keeps up with critical command over essential businesses and areas while permitting markets to work. State-claimed ventures (SOEs) coincide with exclusive organizations, making a crossover monetary framework.

Worldwide Exchange and Multilateral Associations: China effectively participated in worldwide exchange and turned into an individual from global associations like the World Exchange Association (WTO). Its support in worldwide monetary administration permitted it to shape exchange strategies and advantage from global participation.

Difficulties and Concerns

While China's financial ascent has been noteworthy, it has likewise led to a few difficulties and concerns:

Pay Imbalance: Monetary development has not been equitably dispersed in China. Pay imbalance has expanded, with critical incongruities among metropolitan and provincial regions. This has raised social and policy driven issues, as well as worries about friendly security.

Natural Effect: Quick industrialization and urbanization have negatively affected China's current circumstance. Air contamination, water pollution, and deforestation are huge ecological difficulties. China has done whatever it may take to resolve these issues and change to a more practical development model.

Segment Difficulties: China faces segment difficulties, including a maturing populace and a contracting labor force. The one-youngster strategy, which was set up for a very long time, has added to these segment shifts. The nation should address these difficulties to support its financial development.

Obligation and Monetary Dangers: China's financial development has been joined by a significant expansion in the red levels, both in the general population and confidential areas. Overseeing obligation and potential monetary dangers is a vital worry for the Chinese government.

Protected innovation and Innovation Move: China's way to deal with protected innovation freedoms and innovation move has been a subject of conflict in its financial relations with different nations. Worries about protected innovation robbery and constrained innovation moves have incited exchange debates with the US and different countries.

International Pressures: China's monetary ascent has prompted international strains, especially with the US. Exchange debates, security concerns, and contest for worldwide impact have stressed relations between the two superpowers.

Political and Common freedoms Concerns: China's political framework, portrayed by one-party rule, has been reprimanded for its limitations on political dispute and basic liberties. These worries have suggestions for China's worldwide standing and associations with different countries.

The Belt and Street Drive (BRI)

One of the most aggressive and extensive activities related with China's financial ascent is the Belt and Street Drive (BRI). Sent off in 2013, the BRI is a gigantic framework and monetary improvement drive that tries to upgrade network and collaboration among China and nations across Asia, Europe, Africa, and then some.

The BRI comprises of two primary parts:

The Silk Street Monetary Belt: This land-put together part centers with respect to interfacing China with Europe through an organization of overland passageways. These passages envelop street, rail, and pipeline projects that navigate Focal Asia, the Center East, and Eastern Europe.

The 21st Century Oceanic Silk Street: This ocean based part looks to connect China with Southeast Asia, South Asia, Africa, and Europe through an organization of ports and sea framework.

The BRI's goals incorporate advancing exchange, speculation, and monetary turn of events, as well as improving local collaboration. It includes interests in transportation, energy, media communications, and other basic foundation areas.

The BRI can possibly carry monetary advantages to taking an interest nations by working with exchange and foundation improvement. Nonetheless, it has additionally created worries about obligation maintainability, ecological effect, and the potential for international impact.

Worldwide Ramifications

Financial Relationship: China's monetary development has made it a fundamental exchanging accomplice for some nations. As the world's biggest exporter and second-biggest shipper, it is profoundly coordinated into the worldwide economy. Financial association with China has the two advantages and difficulties for different countries.

Change in Monetary Power: China's financial command has prompted a change in worldwide financial power. It has tested the conventional strength of Western economies and has led to a multipolar world.

3.1 China's economic transformation in recent decades

China's financial change in late many years has been perhaps of the most noteworthy and effective improvement in the cutting edge world. From a dominatingly agrarian economy during the twentieth 100 years, China has arisen as a worldwide monetary force to be reckoned with, positioning as the world's second-biggest economy. This change has reshaped the worldwide financial scene, tested standard way of thinking, and ignited inescapable interest and discussion about the variables and elements driving China's phenomenal monetary development.

The seeds of China's financial change were planted in the last part of the 1970s when the nation left on a progression of aggressive monetary changes under the administration of Deng Xiaoping. These changes addressed an unequivocal break from the unbending unified arranging of the Mao period and denoted the start of the "change and opening-up" strategy that changed China's economy.

One of the central changes in financial arrangement was the presentation of the Family Obligation Framework in farming. This change gave ranchers more independence and motivators, permitting them to come to conclusions about what yields to develop and how to apportion their creation. The outcome was a huge expansion in horticultural efficiency, higher expectations for everyday comforts in country regions, and an overflow of rural items that established the groundwork for financial development.

All the while, China started to open its economy to unfamiliar venture and exchange, drawing in unfamiliar capital and mastery to fuel its quick industrialization. Extraordinary Financial Zones (SEZs) were laid out to offer motivations to unfamiliar organizations ready to put and set up activities in China. These zones gave a favorable climate to worldwide organizations, prodding unfamiliar direct speculation (FDI) and the development of product situated ventures.

The change of China's financial scene has been driven by a few key elements:

Assembling and Commodities: China's assembling area turned into the "world's plant." The country's huge workforce, alongside lower creation costs, permitted it to deliver many merchandise at cutthroat costs. This upper hand shot China into a worldwide assembling and trading center.

Unfamiliar Direct Venture (FDI): China effectively looked for unfamiliar speculation, offering motivations and open doors for unfamiliar organizations to lay out a presence in the country. This inundation of FDI brought innovation, aptitude, and capital, adding to China's modern turn of events.

Framework Advancement: China put vigorously in foundation, including a broad organization of streets, rail routes, ports, and air terminals. These framework enhancements worked with homegrown availability, decreased transportation costs, and made the development of products and individuals more effective.

Urbanization: China encountered a gigantic rush of urbanization as individuals moved from provincial regions to urban communities in quest for better financial open doors. This segment shift from agrarian to metropolitan living prompted expanded work efficiency and more noteworthy shopper interest.

Training and Labor force: China put areas of strength for on schooling and put resources into its labor force. Subsequently, the nation fostered a huge pool of profoundly gifted specialists, designers, and researchers who added to mechanical headways and development.

State-Drove Free enterprise: China embraced a special monetary model known as "state-drove private enterprise." Under this model, the state keeps up with critical command over essential businesses and areas, while likewise permitting market influences to work. State-possessed undertakings (SOEs) exist together with exclusive organizations, making a half and half monetary framework.

Worldwide Exchange and Multilateral Associations: China effectively took part in worldwide exchange and turned into an individual from global associations like the World Exchange Association (WTO). Its support in worldwide monetary administration permitted China to impact exchange approaches and advantage from global collaboration.

Development and Innovation: China put vigorously in innovative work, cultivating mechanical headways and advancements in regions like 5G innovation, online business, and man-made consciousness.

China's fast industrialization and commodity situated development technique moved its financial turn of events. The nation set up a good foundation for itself as a worldwide monetary forerunner in different areas, from hardware and materials to assembling and strategies.

In any case, similarly as with any extraordinary excursion, China's financial ascent was joined by difficulties and concerns:

Pay Imbalance: Financial development has not been equally appropriated in China. Pay imbalance has expanded, bringing about critical differences among metropolitan and rustic regions. This has raised social and policy centered issues and worries about friendly steadiness.

Ecological Effect: Fast industrialization and urbanization have negatively affected China's current circumstance. Air contamination, water pollution, and deforestation are critical ecological difficulties. China has put forth attempts to resolve these issues and progress to a more feasible development model.

Segment Difficulties: China faces segment difficulties, including a maturing populace and a contracting labor force. The one-kid strategy, which was set up for quite some time, has added to these segment shifts. The nation should address these difficulties to support its monetary development.

Obligation and Monetary Dangers: China's financial development has been joined by a significant expansion in the red levels, both in the general population and confidential areas. Overseeing obligation and potential monetary dangers is a vital worry for the Chinese government.

Licensed innovation and Innovation Move: China's way to deal with licensed innovation privileges and innovation move has been a subject of conflict in its monetary relations with different nations. Worries about licensed innovation burglary and constrained innovation moves have provoked exchange debates with the US and different countries.

International Pressures: China's financial ascent has prompted international strains, especially with the US. Exchange questions, security concerns, and rivalry for worldwide impact have stressed relations between the two superpowers.

Political and Basic liberties Concerns: China's political framework, portrayed by one-party rule, has been reprimanded for its limitations on political difference and common freedoms. These worries have suggestions for China's global standing and associations with different countries.

One of the most aggressive ventures related with China's financial ascent is the Belt and Street Drive (BRI). Sent off in 2013, the BRI is an enormous framework and financial improvement drive that plans to upgrade network and participation among China and nations across Asia, Europe, Africa, and then some.

The BRI comprises of two primary parts:

The Silk Street Financial Belt: This land-put together part centers with respect to interfacing China with Europe through an organization of overland passageways. These hallways incorporate street, rail, and pipeline projects that cross Focal Asia, the Center East, and Eastern Europe.

The 21st Century Oceanic Silk Street: This ocean based part tries to interface China with Southeast Asia, South Asia, Africa, and Europe by means of an organization of ports and sea framework.

The BRI's goals incorporate advancing exchange, venture, and financial turn of events, as well as improving local participation. It includes interests in transportation, energy, media communications, and other basic framework areas.

The BRI can possibly carry financial advantages to partaking nations by working with exchange and foundation advancement. Nonetheless, it has likewise produced worries about obligation manageability, ecological effect, and the potential for international impact.

China's monetary ascent has significant worldwide ramifications:

Financial Reliance: China's monetary development has made it an essential exchanging accomplice for some nations. As the world's biggest exporter and second-biggest merchant, China is profoundly incorporated into the worldwide economy. Monetary reliance with China has the two advantages and difficulties for different countries.

Change in Financial Power: China's monetary command has prompted a change in worldwide financial power. It has tested the conventional predominance of Western economies and has led to a multipolar world, where a few nations hold critical financial impact.

Innovation and Development: China's interest in innovative work has prompted huge mechanical headways. The nation has turned into a worldwide forerunner in regions like 5G innovation, online business, and man-made consciousness. Its mechanical ability can possibly shape future enterprises and advancement.

International Elements: China's monetary and military ascent has modified the international scene. It has championed itself in provincial and worldwide undertakings and is progressively viewed as a central part in global relations. International strains and fights for control have arisen accordingly.

Worldwide Administration: China's part in global associations and multilateral administration has extended. It is an individual from establishments like the Unified Countries, the World Exchange Association, and the Global Money related Asset. China's impact in these associations has developed, affecting worldwide approaches and navigation.

Worldwide Stock Chains: China's job as the "world's production line" has made it a vital participant in worldwide stock chains. Interruptions, for example, those brought about by the Coronavirus pandemic, have featured the weaknesses and conditions related with this interconnectedness.

The direction of China's financial development before very long will rely upon different variables, including its capacity to address the difficulties it faces and the decisions it makes with regards to monetary arrangement. Some key consideration.

3.2 Government policies and economic reforms

Government strategies and monetary changes assume a basic part in forming the financial scene of a country. They can be instrumental in driving financial development, encouraging advancement, and guaranteeing social prosperity. This conversation will investigate the connection between government strategies and monetary changes, with an emphasis on how they impact a country's financial direction and improvement.

Verifiable Setting of Government Strategies and Financial Changes

Government mediation in the economy is definitely not another idea. Since forever ago, state run administrations play played different parts in forming financial results. The financial way of thinking and way to deal with administration have advanced over the long haul, frequently in light of evolving conditions, philosophical movements, and examples gained from past encounters.

For a significant part of the twentieth hundred years, numerous nations embraced Keynesian financial strategies, which underscored government mediation as monetary and money related measures to balance out and invigorate the economy. In any case, this approach confronted difficulties, especially in managing issues like expansion and stagnation.

In the late twentieth 100 years, another rush of financial reasoning arose, frequently alluded to as neoliberalism or the Washington Agreement. This approach upheld for restricted government mediation, market-arranged changes, liberation, and privatization. The conviction was that unregulated economies, rivalry, and decreased government impedance would prompt more prominent financial effectiveness and flourishing.

Government Arrangements and Financial Turn of events

Government strategies significantly affect a country's financial turn of events. They can establish a climate that encourages or ruins monetary development. The decision of strategy devices, their plan, and their execution can decide the generally financial wellbeing of a country. A few key regions where government strategies impact monetary improvement include:

1. **Financial Strategy:** Monetary arrangement includes government income and consumption choices. Legislatures can utilize tax collection, public spending, and monetary assignments to impact financial results. For instance, expansionary monetary strategies, including tax breaks and expanded government spending, can invigorate financial development during a downturn. Then again, contractionary monetary approaches, with charge climbs and diminished public spending, can assist with controlling expansion and lessen shortfalls.

2. **Financial Approach:** Financial strategy is the space of national banks, which manage the cash supply, loan fees, and the security of monetary foundations. National banks can utilize apparatuses

like open market activities, hold prerequisites, and the rebate rate to control expansion, oversee loan fees, and settle the monetary framework.

3. **Modern Strategy:** States can assume a part in molding the modern and financial construction of a country. They can give impetuses and backing to explicit businesses or areas, empowering development and improvement in essential regions. This approach has been strikingly utilized by nations, for example, South Korea and Japan, which have cultivated the development of enterprises like gadgets and auto producing.

4. **Exchange Strategy:** Government strategies connected with global exchange can essentially influence a country's financial turn of events. Exchange arrangements include duties, shares, economic deals, and product import guidelines. Exchange progression, where state run administrations decrease hindrances to worldwide exchange, can improve financial development by extending market access and encouraging contest.

5. **Work Market Strategies:** Work market arrangements envelop issues like the lowest pay permitted by law regulations, work guidelines, and joblessness benefits. States can shape the work market's elements by establishing strategies that safeguard laborers' privileges and government assistance, support labor force improvement, and guarantee a fair and comprehensive work market.

6. **Training and Medical care:** Government interest in schooling and medical services is critical for human resources improvement and monetary development. Admittance to quality training and medical care administrations can upgrade efficiency, increment a gifted labor force, and work on generally prosperity.

7. **Administrative Climate:** The administrative structure laid out by legislatures can fundamentally impact financial turn of events. An ideal administrative climate can draw in venture, support business, and guarantee purchaser security. Then again, unreasonable or bulky guidelines can smother monetary movement.

Financial Changes

Financial changes are conscious changes to monetary strategies and designs determined to work on financial execution and cultivating development. These changes can be exhaustive, tending to different parts of the economy, or designated at explicit areas or issues. The inspiration for financial changes might shift and can be driven by monetary emergencies, the quest for intensity, or a longing to adjust to changing worldwide monetary circumstances.

A few kinds of financial changes have been executed by states all over the planet:

1. **Liberation:** Liberation includes lessening or taking out unofficial laws and limitations in different areas, like media communications, transportation, and money. The objective is to advance rivalry, decrease boundaries to section, and energize development. For instance, the liberation of the aircraft business in the US in the last part of the 1970s prompted expanded contest and lower airfares.

2. **Privatization:** Privatization includes moving state-claimed endeavors and resources for the confidential area. This strategy is many times sought after to upgrade productivity, decrease government contribution in the economy, and draw in confidential speculation. Outstanding privatization endeavors incorporate the offer of state-possessed undertakings in the Unified Realm during the 1980s.

3. **Exchange Advancement:** Exchange progression envelops lessening levies, standards, and other exchange obstructions. States carry out exchange changes to support worldwide exchange, access worldwide business sectors, and advantage from relative benefits. The Overall Settlement on Duties and Exchange (GATT) and its replacement, the World Exchange Association (WTO), have been instrumental in advancing exchange advancement.

4. **Charge Changes:** Expense changes plan to improve on charge frameworks, lessen taxation rates, and upgrade the productivity and reasonableness of duty assortment. Changes might include changes to personal assessment rates, corporate duties, esteem added charges (Tank), and different types of tax collection.

5. **Monetary Area Changes:** Monetary area changes center around upgrading the solidness and proficiency of monetary business sectors and organizations. Measures might incorporate the foundation of administrative bodies, improvement of banking frameworks, and the presentation of new monetary instruments.

6. **Work Market Changes:** Work market changes try to resolve issues connected with business, work guidelines, and labor force adaptability. These changes can advance work creation, labor force cooperation, and lessen work market rigidities.

7. **Primary Changes:** Underlying changes are thorough changes pointed toward tending to underlying shortcomings in an economy. These changes might include changes in training, medical care, framework, and policy management to improve monetary strength and seriousness.

Monetary Change Examples of overcoming adversity

A few nations have executed fruitful financial changes that significantly affect their monetary turn of events:

China: China's monetary changes, started by Deng Xiaoping in the last part of the 1970s, have been instrumental in changing the country from a shut, halfway arranged economy to a worldwide financial force to be reckoned with. These changes included opening up to unfamiliar speculation, empowering business venture, and making extraordinary financial zones to draw in unfamiliar capital.

India: In 1991, India executed a progression of monetary changes that changed the economy, diminished exchange hindrances, and supported unfamiliar speculation. These changes have added to India's monetary development and rise as a significant worldwide economy.

New Zealand: During the 1980s and 1990s, New Zealand embraced a progression of complete market-situated monetary changes. These changes included financial limitation, liberation, privatization, and exchange progression, which worked on the country's monetary execution.

Singapore: Singapore's financial achievement is credited to a mix of monetary changes that focus on receptiveness, exchange, and venture. These changes have made Singapore one of the world's most aggressive and financially dynamic countries.

Chile: Chile's monetary changes during the 1980s involved changing exchange, privatizing state-claimed undertakings, and encouraging a serious market climate. These changes added to Chile's financial development and dependability.

Difficulties and Contemplations

While financial changes can have huge advantages, they are not without difficulties and possible entanglements. Legislatures should cautiously plan and execute changes to guarantee they line up with the country's monetary and social objectives. A few contemplations and difficulties during the time spent financial changes include:

Social Effect: Changes might have social outcomes, like work uprooting or imbalance. Legislatures should consider systems to moderate these effects, like retraining programs or designated help to weak populaces.

Political Obstruction: Financial changes can confront political opposition from vested parties and partners who might be antagonistically impacted. Building agreement and political will for changes is a basic part of effective execution.

Institutional Limit: Compelling execution of changes frequently major areas of strength for requires, administrative systems, and administration structures. Building and reinforcing these limits can be a complex and tedious interaction.

3.3 Challenges and opportunities for China's continued growth

China's astounding monetary change throughout the course of recent many years has been absolutely remarkable. From being a transcendently agrarian culture during the twentieth hundred years, China has arisen as the world's second-biggest economy, using significant effect on the worldwide stage. Be that as it may, this momentous excursion has likewise delivered a one of a kind arrangement of difficulties and open doors for China's proceeded with development and improvement. In this conversation, we will investigate the multi-layered scene that China faces as it explores the intricacies of its financial future.

Challenges

Segment Movements: China is encountering critical segment difficulties. The country's populace is maturing, and the labor force is contracting. The one-kid strategy, which was set up for a considerable length of time, has added to this segment shift. A maturing populace can strain social government assistance frameworks, and a contracting labor force might influence monetary efficiency.

Pay Disparity: Monetary development in China has not been equitably circulated. Pay imbalance has expanded, with huge incongruities among metropolitan and provincial regions. This has raised social and policy centered issues, as well as worries about friendly security and variations in expectations for everyday comforts.

Ecological Debasement: China's fast industrialization and urbanization have negatively affected the climate. The nation faces difficulties connected with air contamination, water pollution, deforestation, and other natural issues. These difficulties not just have wellbeing and personal satisfaction suggestions yet additionally present long haul monetary dangers.

Obligation Levels: China's monetary development has been joined by a significant expansion under water levels, both in people in general and confidential areas. Overseeing obligation and potential monetary dangers is a vital worry for the Chinese government. High obligation levels can influence financial security and development while perhaps not appropriately made due.

Licensed innovation and Innovation Move: China's way to deal with protected innovation privileges and innovation move has been a subject of conflict in its monetary relations with different nations. Worries about licensed innovation robbery and constrained innovation moves have prompted exchange debates with the US and different countries, making financial and conciliatory pressures.

International Strains: China's monetary ascent has prompted international pressures, especially with the US. Exchange debates, security concerns, and rivalry for worldwide impact have stressed relations between the two superpowers. These pressures have financial ramifications and can disturb global exchange and venture.

Political and Common liberties Concerns: China's political framework, described by one-party rule, has been reprimanded for its limitations on political contradiction and basic freedoms. These worries have suggestions for China's worldwide standing and associations with different countries.

Potential open doors

Homegrown Utilization: China's huge and developing working class presents a critical chance for homegrown utilization. As additional Chinese residents enter the working class, there is a thriving interest for buyer merchandise, administrations, and encounters. This presents a development motor for the economy, decreasing dependence on outer business sectors.

Development and Innovation Administration: China has put vigorously in innovative work, cultivating development and mechanical progressions. The nation means to be a worldwide forerunner in regions like man-made reasoning, 5G innovation, clean energy, and biotechnology. These headways can possibly drive future enterprises and financial development.

Urbanization: The continuous urbanization pattern in China, with a huge number of individuals moving from provincial regions to urban areas, adds to financial development. Urbanization prompts expanded work efficiency, higher purchaser interest, and valuable open doors for land improvement and framework projects.

Worldwide Exchange and Speculation: China's dynamic cooperation in worldwide exchange and venture can possibly drive financial development. The Belt and Street Drive (BRI) is a gigantic framework and financial improvement drive that looks to upgrade network and collaboration among China and nations across Asia, Europe, Africa, and then some. The BRI can cultivate exchange, venture, and monetary turn of events.

Ecological Supportability: China has perceived the significance of addressing natural difficulties and progressing to a more practical development model. Endeavors to lessen contamination, put resources into clean energy, and advance practical improvement relieve natural dangers as well as set out open doors in green businesses.

Worldwide Stockpile Chains: China's job as the "world's production line" makes it a key member in worldwide inventory chains. As worldwide organizations try to differentiate production network sources and decrease gambles, China can draw in more unfamiliar speculation and become a center for cutting edge assembling and innovation.

Worldwide Administration: China's job in global associations and multilateral administration has extended. As an individual from foundations like the Unified Countries, the World Exchange Association, and the Worldwide Financial Asset, China impacts worldwide strategies and direction.

Monetary Area Advancement: China has been bit by bit opening up its monetary area to unfamiliar venture and rivalry. This presents open doors for global monetary organizations to extend their presence in the Chinese market, expanding capital stream and monetary administrations.

The Belt and Street Drive (BRI)

One of the most aggressive and broad ventures related with China's financial ascent is the Belt and Street Drive (BRI). Sent off in 2013, the BRI is a huge foundation and financial improvement drive that means to upgrade network and collaboration among China and nations across Asia, Europe, Africa, and then some.

The BRI comprises of two principal parts:

The Silk Street Monetary Belt: This land-put together part centers with respect to interfacing China with Europe through an organization of overland passageways. These halls incorporate street, rail, and pipeline projects that navigate Focal Asia, the Center East, and Eastern Europe.

The 21st Century Sea Silk Street: This ocean based part looks to connect China with Southeast Asia, South Asia, Africa, and Europe through an organization of ports and sea foundation.

The BRI's targets incorporate advancing exchange, venture, and monetary turn of events, as well as improving provincial participation. It includes interests in transportation, energy, broadcast communications, and other basic framework areas.

The BRI can possibly carry monetary advantages to taking an interest nations by working with exchange and framework improvement. It can likewise set out open doors for Chinese organizations to extend their presence in these districts. Notwithstanding, the drive has created worries about obligation supportability, ecological effect, and the potential for international impact.

4

Chapter 4

Japan: From Post-War Recovery to Technological Pioneer

In the consequence of The Second Great War, Japan confronted an overwhelming undertaking: revamping a country that had been desolated by war and occupation. The obliteration was far and wide, both regarding actual foundation and the country's mind. Notwithstanding, Japan's wonderful change from a crushed and crushed country to a worldwide mechanical trailblazer is an account of strength, development, and immovable assurance.

The prompt post-war time frame in Japan was set apart by a feeling of despondency and destruction. The urban communities lay in ruins, and the economy was wrecked. The 1945 nuclear bombings of Hiroshima and Nagasaki had left an enduring scar on the public cognizance, highlighting the significance of harmony and modifying. Japan was involved by Associated powers, drove by the US, and under the direction of General Douglas MacArthur, the Incomparable Administrator for the Partnered Powers (SCAP), the course of remaking and change started.

One of the most eminent and persevering through traditions of the post-war time was the new Japanese constitution, which became effective in 1947. This constitution, frequently alluded to as the

"Constitution of Japan" or the "Post bellum Constitution," denied Japan's on the whole correct to take up arms, laid out a parliamentary arrangement of government, and revered principal basic liberties. It was a huge takeoff from the pre-war strategic system, underlining vote based standards and pacifism.

The financial recuperation of Japan in the post-war years was completely extraordinary. The public authority and individuals of Japan, with their trademark discipline and ingenuity, set about reconstructing the country. The U.S. offered basic help through the Marshall Plan, which imbued Japan's economy with much-required monetary help. The Keidanren (Japan League of Financial Associations) assumed a focal part in organizing monetary exercises and liaising with the public authority.

Japanese industry was rebuilt and modernized, and new areas like steel, synthetic substances, and cars started to arise as key supporters of the country's financial development. During the 1950s, the Japanese government laid out the Service of Worldwide Exchange and Industry (MITI) to facilitate modern strategy and advance the development of key businesses. MITI assumed a vital part in directing Japan's financial improvement throughout the next many years.

The early post-war time frame likewise saw the rise of enormous business combinations known as keiretsu, which turned into a foundation of Japan's monetary scene. These keiretsu, like the Mitsui, Sumitomo, and Mitsubishi gatherings, were upward coordinated and expanded, assuming a pivotal part in the post-war recuperation by giving capital, skill, and assets.

Japan's commodity situated industrialization system was instrumental in its quick monetary development. The nation zeroed in on delivering superior grade, seriously valued merchandise for global business sectors. The world came to perceive Japan for its accuracy and craftsmanship in different enterprises, from gadgets to cars. Organizations like Toyota, Honda, Sony, and Panasonic became commonly recognized names all over the planet.

The 1964 Tokyo Olympics were a vital second for Japan, displaying the country's wonderful advancement and recuperation. The Olympics were viewed as an image of Japan's change from a conflict torn country to a financial and mechanical force to be reckoned with. The occasion additionally saw the presentation of the Shinkansen, or slug train, which exemplified Japan's obligation to state of the art framework and innovation.

Japan's mechanical headways during this period were not restricted to transportation. The nation quickly arose as a forerunner in hardware and media communications. Organizations like Sony and Toshiba became inseparable from development and quality. The Sony Walkman, presented in 1979, upset individual sound, while Toshiba's commitments to semiconductor innovation were momentous.

The 1970s and 1980s denoted Japan's rising in the worldwide economy, with the nation accomplishing wonderful development rates. Japan's auto industry, specifically, came to rule global business sectors. The "Japanese marvel" was described by serious areas of strength for an ethic, effective creation techniques, and a persevering spotlight on quality.

Japan's ascent, be that as it may, was not without discussion. Allegations of unreasonable exchange rehearses, for example, unloading and cash control, prompted exchange questions with the US and different countries. The Court Accord of 1985 meant to address Japan's enormous exchange excess by valuing the yen, which diminished Japan's seriousness in worldwide business sectors.

The blasting of Japan's financial air pocket in the mid 1990s denoted a defining moment in the country's monetary direction. The "Lost 10 years" that followed saw delayed monetary stagnation, a deflationary twisting, and a financial emergency. This period was portrayed by lazy development and resource value flattening, and it presented critical difficulties to Japan's economy.

While Japan's monetary supernatural occurrence had been driven by its product situated development model, the drawn out financial discomfort constrained the country to search for better approaches to invigorate homegrown interest.

The public authority carried out different financial improvement measures and banking area changes, however recuperation stayed tricky.

The 21st century brought new open doors and difficulties for Japan. The nation kept on putting resources into innovative work, cultivating advancement in fields like mechanical technology, biotechnology, and sustainable power. Japan's obligation to mechanical progression was exhibited with the send off of the Hayabusa mission, which effectively returned tests from a space rock in 2010.

The Fukushima Daiichi atomic debacle in 2011 was a significant difficulty, for Japan as well as for the worldwide atomic industry. The episode, set off by a huge quake and tidal wave, prompted the arrival of radioactive materials and a reexamination of Japan's dependence on atomic power. The public authority thusly reported a change in energy strategy, underlining sustainable power sources and diminishing atomic power's part in the energy blend.

Japan's segment difficulties additionally came to the very front in the 21st hundred years. The nation confronted a quickly maturing populace and declining rates of birth. The public authority acquainted arrangements with address these issues, including motivators for families to have more kids and measures to advance the dynamic support of older residents in the labor force.

As Japan explored its direction through the 21st 100 years, it kept on assuming a critical part on the worldwide stage. The nation effectively partook in global strategy and compassionate endeavors, and it stayed resolved to its post-war radical constitution. Japan additionally developed close financial binds with adjoining nations in Asia, adding to the locale's monetary development and steadiness.

Japan's devotion to mechanical development was exemplified by the improvement of humanoid robots and progressions in man-made consciousness. The nation was at the cutting edge of exploration in these fields, with organizations like SoftBank, Toyota, and Honda putting vigorously in mechanical technology and computerization advancements.

The Tokyo 2020 Olympics, delayed to 2021 because of the Coronavirus pandemic, were a demonstration of Japan's flexibility and obligation to facilitating the worldwide occasion in spite of phenomenal difficulties. The Olympics exhibited Japan's state of the art innovation and foundation while featuring the soul of solidarity and diligence.

As of late, Japan has additionally taken huge steps in space investigation. The fruitful missions of the Hayabusa2 shuttle, which gathered examples from the space rock Ryugu, and the send off of the Kibo module on the Worldwide Space Station showed Japan's capacities in space science and innovation.

Japan's worldwide impact stretched out past financial matters and innovation. The nation stayed a forerunner in natural preservation and economical practices. Japanese organizations created progressed eco-accommodating advances, and Japan was effectively associated with global endeavors to battle environmental change.

Japan's social impact kept on resounding around the world, with anime, manga, and Japanese food getting a charge out of far reaching fame. The "Cool Japan" drive tried to advance Japanese culture and inventiveness all around the world, further upgrading the country's delicate power.

4.1 Japan's recovery after World War II

The finish of The Second Great War left Japan in a condition of pulverization, both truly and inwardly. The country had been significantly impacted by the contention, and the prompt post-war time frame was set apart by huge difficulties and the requirement for an extensive recuperation. The tale of Japan's recuperation from the cinders of battle to turning into a worldwide monetary and mechanical force to be reckoned with is a demonstration of the flexibility and assurance of its kin, as well as the effect of cautious preparation and global collaboration.

The pulverization of Japan following The Second Great War was broad. The nation's significant urban communities lay in ruins, and its economy was shredded. The nuclear bombings of Hiroshima and Nagasaki in 1945 had left an enduring scar on the public cognizance, underscoring the significance of harmony and reconstructing. Japan was involved by Unified powers, with General Douglas MacArthur as the Preeminent Authority for the Partnered Powers (SCAP) directing the reproduction and change endeavors.

One of the most critical and enduring changes during this period was the reception of another Japanese constitution, which became effective in 1947. Frequently alluded to as the "Constitution of Japan" or the "Post bellum Constitution," it repudiated Japan's on the right track to take up arms, laid out a parliamentary arrangement of government, and revered basic common liberties. This constitution denoted a huge take-off from the pre-war strategic system, putting areas of strength for an on just standards and pacifism.

Japan's financial recuperation during the post-war years was out and out astounding. The Japanese government and its kin, known for their discipline and constancy, left on the fantastic assignment of re-making the country. The US offered pivotal help through the Marshall Plan, infusing truly necessary monetary help into Japan's economy. The Keidanren, or Japan League of Financial Associations, assumed a focal part in planning monetary exercises and going about as a delegate with the public authority.

Japanese industry went through a change, modernizing and re-building to line up with post-war monetary real factors. Arising areas like steel, synthetic substances, and vehicles became key drivers of the country's monetary development.

During the 1950s, the Japanese government laid out the Service of Global Exchange and Industry (MITI) to arrange modern strategy and advance the improvement of key ventures. MITI assumed a urgent part in directing Japan's financial improvement in the many years that followed.

The early post-war time frame likewise saw the rise of huge business aggregates known as keiretsu, which became indispensable to Japan's financial scene. These keiretsu, like the Mitsui, Sumitomo, and Mitsubishi gatherings, were upward coordinated and expanded, giving basic capital, mastery, and assets to help the country's recuperation.

Japan's commodity situated industrialization system was a foundation of its quick financial development. The nation zeroed in on delivering superior grade, seriously estimated merchandise for global business sectors, and the world before long perceived Japan for its accuracy and craftsmanship in different ventures, from hardware to autos. Organizations like Toyota, Honda, Sony, and Panasonic became worldwide easily recognized names.

The 1964 Tokyo Olympics denoted an essential second for Japan, filling in as an image of the country's momentous advancement and recuperation. The Olympics displayed Japan's change from a conflict torn country to a monetary and innovative force to be reckoned with. The occasion likewise presented the Shinkansen, or shot train, featuring Japan's obligation to state of the art foundation and innovation.

Japan's innovative progressions during this period reached out past transportation. The nation quickly arose as a forerunner in hardware and broadcast communications. Organizations like Sony and Toshiba became inseparable from advancement and quality. The presentation of the Sony Walkman in 1979 reformed individual sound, and Toshiba's commitments to semiconductor innovation were noteworthy.

The 1970s and 1980s saw Japan's climb in the worldwide economy, portrayed by amazing development rates. Japan's auto industry, specifically, overwhelmed worldwide business sectors. The "Japanese marvel" was powered by areas of strength for an ethic, effective creation techniques, and a steadfast obligation to quality.

In any case, Japan's monetary ascent was not without debate. Allegations of out of line exchange rehearses, for example, unloading and cash control, prompted exchange debates with the US and different countries. The Court Accord of 1985 expected to address Japan's significant exchange excess by valuing the yen, which decreased Japan's seriousness in worldwide business sectors.

The blasting of Japan's monetary air pocket in the mid 1990s denoted a defining moment in the country's financial direction. The "Lost 10 years" that followed was described by delayed monetary stagnation, a deflationary winding, and a financial emergency. This period saw languid development and resource cost flattening, presenting critical difficulties to Japan's economy.

Japan's financial supernatural occurrence had been driven by its product situated development model, however the delayed monetary discomfort constrained the country to look for better approaches to invigorate homegrown interest. The public authority carried out different monetary boost measures and banking area changes, however recuperation stayed subtle.

The 21st century brought both new open doors and difficulties for Japan. The nation kept on putting resources into innovative work, encouraging development in fields like advanced mechanics, biotechnology, and sustainable power. Japan's obligation to mechanical progression was exhibited by the fruitful Hayabusa mission, which gathered examples from a space rock in 2010.

The Fukushima Daiichi atomic fiasco in 2011 was a significant misfortune, for Japan as well as for the worldwide atomic industry. Set off by a monstrous tremor and wave, the occurrence brought about the arrival of radioactive materials and a reconsideration of Japan's dependence on atomic power. The public authority declared a change in energy strategy, underscoring sustainable power sources and decreasing atomic power's part in the energy blend.

Japan's segment difficulties likewise came to the front in the 21st 100 years. The nation wrestled with a quickly maturing populace and declining rates of birth. The public authority acquainted strategies with address these issues, including impetuses for families to have more kids and measures to empower the dynamic cooperation of older residents in the labor force.

As Japan explored its direction through the 21st 100 years, it kept on assuming a huge part on the worldwide stage. The nation effectively partook in global strategy and helpful endeavors, staying resolved to its post-war conservative constitution. Japan developed close monetary binds with adjoining nations in Asia, adding to the locale's financial development and solidness.

Japan's commitment to mechanical advancement was apparent in the improvement of humanoid robots and progressions in man-made brainpower. The nation was at the bleeding edge of examination in these fields, with organizations like SoftBank, Toyota, and Honda putting vigorously in mechanical technology and computerization advances.

The Tokyo 2020 Olympics, delayed to 2021 because of the Coronavirus pandemic, were a demonstration of Japan's versatility and obligation to facilitating the worldwide occasion notwithstanding extraordinary difficulties. The Olympics exhibited Japan's state of the art innovation and foundation while featuring the soul of solidarity and diligence.

Lately, Japan has likewise taken critical steps in space investigation. The fruitful missions of the Hayabusa2 shuttle, which gathered examples from the space rock Ryugu, and the send off of the Kibo module on the Global Space Station showed Japan's capacities in space science and innovation.

Japan's worldwide impact reached out past financial aspects and innovation. The nation stayed a forerunner in ecological protection and reasonable practices. Japanese organizations created progressed eco-accommodating advances, and Japan was effectively associated with worldwide endeavors to battle environmental change.

Japan's social impact kept on reverberating around the world, with anime, manga, and Japanese cooking appreciating broad ubiquity. The "Cool Japan" drive tried to advance Japanese culture and innovativeness internationally, further improving the country's delicate power.

Notwithstanding its amazing accomplishments and recuperation from the staggering repercussions of The Second Great War, Japan kept on confronting its portion of difficulties in the 21st hundred years. The country's capacity to adjust to evolving conditions, keep up with its obligation to harmony and development, and address segment and natural issues will assume a significant part in molding its future. Japan's excursion from present conflict recuperation on turning into a worldwide monetary and mechanical trailblazer fills in as a helpful story of strength, development, and steady assurance.

4.2 The role of innovation and technological advancements

Development and mechanical headways have for some time been essential drivers of cultural advancement and financial development. The constant improvement of new innovations, alongside their mix into different parts of our lives, has altogether molded the manner in which we live, work, and connect with the world. Throughout the long term, advancement has reformed enterprises, changed economies, and achieved remarkable degrees of comfort, productivity, and network. In this story, we will investigate the complex job of development and mechanical progressions, from their verifiable importance to their contemporary pertinence.

Authentic Importance:

Over the entire course of time, advancement and mechanical headways play had a critical impact in human turn of events and progress. The historical backdrop of advancement can be followed back to the earliest long periods of humankind, as our progenitors found and created instruments to make their lives more straightforward. The wheel, horticulture, and metallurgy were a portion of the early developments that reformed old social orders and stamped critical defining moments in mankind's set of experiences.

In the cutting edge time, the Modern Upheaval of the eighteenth and nineteenth hundreds of years remains as a groundbreaking period in which development and mechanical headways profoundly impacted the world. Steam motors, motorized material creation, and the multiplication of the plant framework introduced a time of extraordinary industrialization, driving monetary development and urbanization.

The job of mechanical progressions was additionally critical in forming the course of The Second Great War. Advancements in avionics, like the improvement of fly motors and radar innovation, altered fighting. Besides, the nuclear bomb, a result of logical and mechanical development, showed both the mind blowing force of human creativity and the potential for disastrous outcomes.

The post-The Second Great War time frame saw the fast advancement of figuring innovation, with the development of the semiconductor and the ensuing ascent of the data age. The development of advanced PCs and the web in the last 50% of the twentieth century altered correspondence, data dispersal, and the manner in which organizations worked.

Monetary Development and Industry Change:

Development and innovative headways have been key drivers of monetary development and industry change. The reception of new advancements frequently prompts expanded efficiency and proficiency, bringing about the production of new business sectors and ventures. For example, the improvement of the vehicle upset transportation, leading to the auto business, which, thusly, cultivated the development of related areas like petrol and foundation advancement.

The innovation area itself has been a great representation of this peculiarity. The approach of PCs in the late twentieth century set out open doors for programming improvement, prompting the development of tech goliaths like Microsoft and Apple. In ongoing many years, the expansion of the web and the ascent of computerized stages have brought forth another age of tech organizations, like Amazon, Google, and Facebook, which have reclassified how we associate, consume data, and lead business.

The job of development in monetary development is exemplified by the idea of "imaginative obliteration," presented by business analyst Joseph Schumpeter. This hypothesis recommends that advancement and innovative advancement drive monetary improvement by delivering old advancements and plans of action outdated, clearing a path for new and more productive ones. While this cycle can be problematic, it eventually prompts expanded success and higher expectations for everyday comforts.

Influence on Schooling and Work:

Development and innovative headways have changed the instruction and work scenes. The joining of innovation in schooling has set out new open doors for remote learning, customized guidance, and admittance to instructive assets. The web has made it feasible for people to seek after internet based courses and degrees, no matter what their geographic area, in this way democratizing admittance to schooling.

In the work environment, innovation significantly affects the idea of work itself. Computerization and man-made consciousness (simulated intelligence) can possibly perform routine errands more effectively than people, prompting conversations about the eventual fate of work and the job of human specialists.

While some trepidation work dislodging, others accept that innovation will set out new open doors and occupations in arising fields connected with simulated intelligence, advanced mechanics, and information science.

The gig economy, portrayed by transient agreements and independent work, has been empowered by advanced stages that interface laborers with managers. The ascent of working from home and remote work game plans, advanced by the Coronavirus pandemic, has additionally changed the conventional office climate and considered more prominent adaptability in how and where work is directed.

Medical care and Clinical Advances:

Development and mechanical headways significantly affect the field of medical services and medication. The advancement of clinical imaging innovations, like X-beams, X-rays, and CT checks, has changed diagnostics and patient consideration. Also, headways in careful methods, including negligibly obtrusive methodology and automated a medical procedure, have worked on the accuracy and results of clinical mediations.

The mix of information investigation and electronic wellbeing records has upgraded medical services conveyance and patient administration. Telemedicine and telehealth stages have extended admittance to medical care administrations, especially in remote or underserved regions. Versatile wellbeing applications and wearable gadgets furnish people with instruments to screen their wellbeing, advancing preventive consideration and patient commitment.

Biotechnology and genomics have opened new wildernesses in customized medication and medication advancement. The capacity to examine a person's hereditary cosmetics takes into account custom fitted treatment plans and the distinguishing proof of hereditary elements related with illnesses. Moreover, the improvement of antibodies and treatments, for example, the fast production of mRNA immunizations for Coronavirus, features the force of advancement in tending to worldwide wellbeing challenges.

Natural Supportability:

Development and mechanical headways play a basic part in tending to ecological difficulties and advancing supportability. The exhaustion of normal assets, environmental change, and natural corruption have provoked a worldwide shift toward additional feasible practices and innovations.

Environmentally friendly power sources, including sun based, wind, and hydropower, have acquired unmistakable quality as options in contrast to petroleum products. Headways in energy capacity advancements, like lithium-particle batteries, have worked on the dependability and practicality of sustainable power frameworks. Developments in electric vehicles (EVs) have additionally diminished ozone depleting substance outflows in the transportation area.

The advancement of manageable structure materials and development rehearses has prompted the production of eco-accommodating and energy-proficient structures. In addition, advancements in wastewater treatment and reusing have assisted save with watering assets and lessen contamination. Roundabout economy models, underlining the reuse and reusing of materials, are building up some forward momentum as a way to diminish squander and limit natural effect.

Social Availability and Correspondence:

Development and mechanical headways have reformed social network and correspondence. The coming of the web and the expansion of online entertainment stages have essentially modified how people communicate with each other and access data. Long range interpersonal communication locales like Facebook, Twitter, and Instagram have changed the manner in which individuals associate, share encounters, and remain informed about recent developments.

The ascent of portable innovation and cell phones has made correspondence more available and helpful. Individuals can discuss right away with people from around the world, rising above topographical and fleeting limits. Video conferencing stages, like Zoom and Skype, have worked with far off gatherings and virtual cooperations, assuming a urgent part in business, training, and unique interactions.

The web has likewise engaged people to make and share content, prompting the development of content makers, bloggers, and powerhouses. Web-based entertainment and computerized stages have democratized media creation and conveyance, empowering a more different and decentralized data scene.

Challenges and Moral Contemplations:

While development and mechanical progressions offer various advantages, they likewise present a scope of difficulties and moral contemplations. One of the essential worries is the effect of innovation on protection and information security. The assortment and scattering of individual data by organizations and states have brought up issues about individual privileges and the potential for reconnaissance and information breaks.

Mechanization and artificial intelligence have raised worries about work dislodging and financial imbalance. As normal errands become robotized, people in specific businesses might confront joblessness or pay stagnation. Guaranteeing that the advantages of development are fairly disseminated and that uprooted laborers approach retraining and schooling is a basic cultural test.

Moral contemplations in computer based intelligence and AI additionally spin around issues of predisposition and segregation. Calculations can sustain predispositions present in preparing information, prompting inconsistent treatment in regions like law enforcement, loaning, and employing. Tending to algorithmic predisposition and guaranteeing decency in man-made intelligence frameworks are continuous needs.

Furthermore, the fast speed of mechanical change has presented difficulties for administrative structures and moral rules. Policymakers frequently battle to stay up with the improvement of new technological.

4.3 The impact of Japanese industries on the global economy

Japanese ventures play had a huge impact in molding the worldwide economy throughout the course of recent many years. Japan's ascent as a monetary force to be reckoned with, especially in areas like car, hardware, and assembling, has had expansive impacts on the world's financial scene. This account investigates the effect of Japanese enterprises on the worldwide economy, from their post-The Second Great War recuperation to their proceeded with impact in different areas.

Post-The Second Great War Recuperation and Monetary Development:

Following The Second Great War, Japan confronted the tremendous undertaking of modifying a country desolated by struggle. The country's urban communities lay in ruins, and its economy was wrecked. Nonetheless, Japan's striking recuperation from decimation was driven by its enterprises and their steady obligation to development, quality, and proficiency.

Key enterprises like steel, synthetics, and vehicles turned into the mainstays of Japan's monetary development during the post-war years. Japanese organizations, including Toyota, Nissan, and Honda, secured themselves as worldwide forerunners in the auto area. The Toyota Creation Framework, with its accentuation on in the nick of time fabricating and consistent improvement, set new principles for effectiveness and quality in the business.

Japanese makers' devotion to accuracy and craftsmanship brought about the creation of top notch merchandise that were seriously valued for worldwide business sectors. Japan's commodities became inseparable from unwavering quality and development, making the "Made in Japan" name a sign of greatness.

Hardware and Mechanical Headways:

Japanese hardware and innovation organizations made huge commitments to the worldwide economy. Firms like Sony, Toshiba, and Panasonic became pioneers in their particular fields, delivering state of the art items that found their direction into families around the world. The Walkman, presented by Sony in 1979, upset individual sound, and Toshiba's headways in semiconductor innovation were momentous.

The 1980s and 1990s saw Japan's predominance in buyer hardware, with items like VCRs, camcorders, and compact Cd players catching global business sectors. Japanese organizations were at the front line of development, starting precedents in scaling down, show innovation, and advanced imaging. They laid out Japan as a center point for innovative work, which added to mechanical progressions in the more extensive worldwide hardware industry.

The Auto Business' Worldwide Effect:

The Japanese car industry's effect on the worldwide economy couldn't possibly be more significant. Japanese automakers presented another degree of productivity and quality to the area, always having an impact on how vehicles were planned, delivered, and showcased. Brands like Toyota, Honda, and Nissan changed the worldwide auto scene, increasing current standards for execution, unwavering quality, and eco-friendliness.

The Japanese automakers' attention on ceaseless improvement and advancement was obvious in their advancement of half and half and electric vehicles. Toyota's presentation of the Prius in 1997 denoted a critical achievement in the reception of cross breed innovation, prompting a more extensive pattern toward additional harmless to the ecosystem vehicles universally.

Japanese automakers likewise exhibited their obligation to creation proficiency through the spread of "in the nick of time" fabricating procedures and lean creation systems. These methodologies decreased costs as well as filled in as models for organizations overall hoping to further develop their assembling processes.

Producing Greatness:

Japan's assembling area has for some time been respected for its proficiency and quality. The standards of "kaizen" (persistent improvement) and "jidoka" (mechanization with a human touch) have become essential to the way of thinking of Japanese assembling. This emphasis on greatness has permitted Japanese enterprises to stay cutthroat on a worldwide scale.

The "5S" system — Sort, Put together, Sparkle, Normalize, Maintain — underscores working environment association and neatness, making a culture of proficiency and efficiency. Japanese assembling rehearses are utilized as benchmarks for organizations all over the planet trying to smooth out their tasks and upgrade item quality.

Impact on Supply Chains:

Japanese enterprises play had a pivotal impact in forming worldwide stock chains. The "in the nick of time" stock administration framework, spearheaded by Toyota, has turned into a foundation of store network the executives. It accentuates delivering just what is required, when it is required, diminishing stock expenses, and limiting waste.

Japanese organizations have likewise embraced the idea of "keiretsu," which includes affectionate connections between producers, providers, and merchants. These connections advance long haul joint effort and dependability inside supply chains, guaranteeing the smooth progression of materials and items.

Global Extension:

Japanese ventures have affected the worldwide economy through sends out as well as put vigorously in unfamiliar business sectors. Japanese automakers, for instance, laid out assembling plants in the US and different nations, adding to work creation and monetary development in those locales.

Japanese gadgets organizations likewise settled a worldwide presence, with assembling offices and innovative work habitats in different nations. This worldwide extension has empowered these organizations to take care of nearby business sectors while additionally adding to the advancement of worldwide stockpile chains.

Challenges and Monetary Movements:

In spite of its significant effect on the worldwide economy, Japan has confronted difficulties that have affected its financial direction. The blasting of Japan's monetary air pocket in the mid 1990s denoted a defining moment, prompting a time of delayed financial stagnation known as the "Lost Ten years." This period was described by drowsy development and resource cost emptying, presenting critical difficulties to Japan's economy.

Besides, Japan's segment difficulties have been a worry. The nation faces a quickly maturing populace and declining rates of birth, which could influence its workforce and monetary development potential. To resolve these issues, the public authority has executed strategies to energize family development and the dynamic cooperation of old residents in the labor force.

Mechanical Headways and Development:

Japanese ventures have kept on driving mechanical progressions and development in the 21st hundred years. Japan's obligation to innovative work has cultivated leap forwards in fields like advanced mechanics, biotechnology, and sustainable power. The nation is perceived for its authority in humanoid robots, with organizations like SoftBank, Toyota, and Honda putting vigorously in mechanical technology and computerization advances.

Japan's space investigation endeavors have additionally acquired worldwide approval. The Hayabusa2 mission, which effectively gathered examples from the space rock Ryugu, showed Japan's capacities in space science and innovation. The country's progressions in space innovation can possibly affect both logical examination and business space investigation.

Natural Drives:

Japan's businesses have effectively sought after natural protection and reasonable practices. The improvement of eco-accommodating innovations and maintainable assembling processes has been really important. Japan has additionally been effectively associated with worldwide endeavors to battle environmental change and decrease ozone depleting substance discharges.

Japanese organizations have driven the way in creating and advancing green advancements. Sustainable power sources, for example, sun based and wind power, have been embraced, and Japan has made huge interests in energy-effective and manageable framework. Endeavors to diminish squander and elevate reusing have added to a more maintainable and ecologically cognizant assembling area.

Social Impact and Delicate Power:

Japanese ventures have added to the country's social impact around the world. Japanese anime, manga, and food have become worldwide peculiarities, forming mainstream society and diversion. The "Cool Japan" drive tries to advance Japanese culture and imagination internationally, upgrading the country's delicate power and social effect.

The impact of Japanese businesses on the worldwide economy is obvious, as they have set benchmarks for productivity, quality, and development across different areas. The car, hardware, and assembling enterprises, specifically, have left an enduring inheritance, changing the manner in which organizations work and items are planned and delivered.

The Worldwide Importance of Japanese Businesses Today:

As we shift focus over to the current day, Japanese enterprises remain exceptionally important in the worldwide economy. The car area keeps on being a critical player, with Japanese automakers spearheading electric and cross breed innovations. Also, Japan's obligation to quality and accuracy keeps on setting worldwide principles, affecting enterprises like purchaser gadgets, semiconductors, and hardware.

Japan's ability in advanced mechanics and computerization is especially pertinent in the ongoing time, as robotization and man-made reasoning keep on molding ventures and labor force elements. Japanese organizations' interest in innovative work positions them as pioneers in the improvement of state of the art advances.

Japanese ventures have likewise shown versatility and flexibility even with financial difficulties. The country's reaction to the blasting of the financial air pocket during the 1990s, as well as its obligation to resolving segment issues and advancing reasonable practices, delineates its capacity to explore complex monetary and cultural difficulties.

Chapter 5

Germany: Precision Engineering and Manufacturing Excellence

Germany has for quite some time been commended for its accuracy designing and assembling greatness, remaining as a worldwide innovator in these fields for a long time. The country's obligation to quality, advancement, and effectiveness has contributed not exclusively to its monetary achievement yet additionally to its impact on different enterprises around the world. This story dives into the authentic and contemporary meaning of German designing and assembling, from its foundations in craftsmanship to its ongoing job in forming the worldwide scene.

Verifiable Establishments:

The foundations of Germany's designing and assembling ability can be followed back to major areas of strength for its of craftsmanship and specialized advancement. In the nineteenth 100 years, Germany was at the front of industrialization, with prominent commitments in fields like apparatus, materials, and synthetic substances. The foundation of famous colleges and examination organizations, like the Technische Universität München and the Fraunhofer Society, laid the preparation for logical and mechanical progressions.

The late nineteenth and mid twentieth hundreds of years saw the development of famous German organizations that would come to characterize the country's designing greatness. Firms like Siemens, Bosch, and Krupp were instrumental in driving development in regions like electrical designing, car innovation, and weighty industry. These organizations displayed areas of strength for a to quality and exploration driven item improvement, becoming foundations of the German economy.

Auto Greatness:

One of the most conspicuous instances of Germany's assembling ability is its car industry. German automakers, including Volkswagen, BMW, Daimler AG (the parent organization of Mercedes-Benz), and Audi, are famous for creating elite execution, accuracy designed vehicles. The "Made in Germany" mark is inseparable from quality, craftsmanship, and designing greatness.

The German auto area has reliably pushed the limits of development, presenting weighty advances that have reshaped the business. Advancements in motor effectiveness, wellbeing highlights, and execution have set worldwide benchmarks. The Expressway, Germany's high velocity thruway organization, is known for its unlimited stretches where drivers can push their vehicles as far as possible, mirroring the country's obligation to designing greatness.

German automakers have additionally embraced supportability, with the improvement of electric and half breed vehicles. Organizations like Volkswagen and BMW have made significant interests in electric portability, tending to the requirement for harmless to the ecosystem transportation and driving worldwide patterns toward jolt.

Designing and Apparatus:

Germany's accuracy designing stretches out past the car business, incorporating an extensive variety of hardware and gear. The nation is a main maker of machine instruments, robotization frameworks, and modern robots. German-made machines are profoundly respected for their accuracy, unwavering quality, and strength.

The "Industry 4.0" drive, which advances the joining of computerized advances into assembling processes, has built up momentum in Germany. It underscores the utilization of computerization, information trade, and man-made reasoning to improve fabricating proficiency and efficiency. The country's aptitude in modern mechanization and advanced mechanics has been compelling in molding the fate of assembling.

The Mittelstand:

A vital component of Germany's assembling scene is the "Mittelstand," a term alluding to little and medium-sized undertakings (SMEs) that are many times family-possessed and zeroed in on specialty markets. These organizations structure the foundation of the German economy, contributing fundamentally to advancement, products, and business. The Mittelstand is known for its versatility, flexibility, and capacity to give particular, top notch items.

Mittelstand firms frequently act as providers to bigger partnerships and assume an imperative part in Germany's stockpile chains. They keep up with cozy associations with clients and focus on long haul organizations, accentuating quality, dependability, and constant improvement. Their obligation to craftsmanship and advancement has made them central participants in Germany's assembling environment.

Quality Guidelines and Accreditation:

Germany puts serious areas of strength for an on quality guidelines and confirmation in its assembling processes. The Racket (Deutsches Institut für Normung) guidelines, laid out in the mid twentieth 100 years, play had a basic impact in directing item quality and guaranteeing consistency. The ISO (Worldwide Association for Normalization) principles, generally perceived and utilized universally, are established in the Commotion framework.

German assembling organizations stick to severe quality control measures, guaranteeing that items fulfill or surpass industry guidelines. The quest for quality is profoundly imbued in the way of life of German designing, and organizations focus on the utilization of cutting edge materials, accuracy machining, and thorough testing to accomplish the most noteworthy potential norms.

Worldwide Products and Exchange:

Germany's assembling and designing ability has made it one of the world's driving commodity economies. German items, from cars to apparatus, are sought after around the world, contributing altogether to the country's monetary strength. The nation's products incorporate many areas, including synthetic compounds, drugs, and modern gear.

Germany's situation as a product force to be reckoned with can be credited to its obligation to quality, accuracy, and development. Its designing firms and producers have utilized these qualities to fabricate durable associations with organizations and clients in different nations. German-made items are much of the time seen as a characteristic of greatness and unwavering quality.

Innovative work:

Germany's administration in designing and assembling is intently attached to its obligation to innovative work (Research and development). The nation's colleges and examination establishments reliably rank among the best around the world, and they effectively team up with industry to drive mechanical headways.

The Fraunhofer Society, for example, is Europe's biggest application-arranged research association. It works intimately with organizations to foster state of the art innovations and address complex designing difficulties. Coordinated effort among the scholarly world and industry guarantees that exploration discoveries are converted into reasonable applications, adding to Germany's standing for development.

Natural Maintainability:

German designing and assembling have embraced the developing accentuation on natural maintainability. Organizations in the auto, hardware, and energy areas have put resources into growing harmless to the ecosystem advancements and decreasing their carbon impression.

In the car business, endeavors to further develop eco-friendliness, diminish discharges, and change to electric versatility have been outstanding. German automakers have fostered a great many crossover and electric vehicles, setting industry guidelines for manageability. This responsibility lines up with worldwide patterns toward cleaner transportation arrangements.

Effect on the European Association:

Germany's solid assembling and designing areas impressively affect the European Association's economy. The nation isn't unquestionably the biggest economy in the EU yet in addition fills in as a center for exchange and modern creation. German assembling contributes essentially to the monetary dependability of the whole EU.

Germany's authority in advancing quality and advancement has impacted the EU's administrative and modern guidelines. The country's solid support for a powerful modern base and maintainable practices has helped shape EU strategies and rules.

Difficulties and Future Viewpoint:

Notwithstanding its striking achievement, Germany's assembling and designing areas face a few difficulties. A maturing populace and a declining rate of birth are worries that might affect the accessibility of gifted work from here on out. The Mittelstand, specifically, may find it trying to draw in and hold ability, requiring systems to address these segment shifts.

Worldwide financial and international vulnerabilities likewise present difficulties. Taxes, exchange questions, and changes in worldwide exchange elements can possibly affect Germany's commodity subordinate economy. Additionally, the Coronavirus pandemic has highlighted the requirement for more prominent flexibility in supply chains, calling for imaginative answers for relieve disturbances.

The designing and assembling areas in Germany keep on developing, with a rising spotlight on digitalization, robotization, and the coordination of shrewd advancements. Industry 4.0 drives are driving the reception of cutting edge producing processes, including the utilization of the Web of Things (IoT), large information examination, and man-made consciousness. These advancements plan to improve creation proficiency, item customization, and adaptability.

5.1 The German model of economic success

The German financial model is many times hailed as a worldview of success and security. Described by serious areas of strength for a base, a talented labor force, an emphasis on development, and a powerful friendly wellbeing net, this model has contributed fundamentally to Germany's getting through financial achievement. This account investigates the critical components of the German financial model, its authentic development, and its contemporary importance in the worldwide scene.

Verifiable Establishments:

Germany's financial achievement can be followed back to its post-The Second Great War recreation and the resulting "Wirtschaftswunder" or monetary supernatural occurrence. In the consequence of the conflict, Germany confronted destruction and crumbling, however its kin and establishments showed exceptional versatility in reconstructing the country. The Marshall Plan gave fundamental monetary help, and the cash change of 1948 laid out the Deutsche Imprint, which established the groundwork for a steady and strong financial framework.

The early long stretches of the Government Republic of Germany saw major areas of strength for a to showcase based free enterprise with a social heart. This methodology, known as the "Social Market Economy" (Soziale Marktwirtschaft), was formed by the main Chancellor of West Germany, Ludwig Erhard. It expected to join unregulated economy standards with a pledge to social government assistance, making ready for the country's noteworthy monetary climb.

Assembling and Product Direction:

At the core of the German financial model is a considerable assembling area. German organizations, frequently alluded to as the "Mittelstand," are a crucial piece of this financial motor. The Mittelstand contains little and medium-sized undertakings (SMEs) that have some expertise in specialty markets, delivering excellent labor and products.

Germany's assembling strength stretches out to a great many ventures, including hardware, car, synthetic substances, and designing. The car area, including organizations like Volkswagen, BMW, Daimler AG (Mercedes-Benz), and Audi, is all around the world eminent for creating elite execution vehicles known for their accuracy and development. The commodity of these vehicles essentially adds to Germany's exchange balance.

Notwithstanding vehicles, hardware and designing items have been a foundation of German assembling greatness. German-made apparatus, gear, and instruments are praised for their quality and dependability. The nation's commodity situated assembling area, joined with an emphasis on development, positions Germany as a worldwide forerunner in industry.

Gifted Labor force and Professional Preparation:

A profoundly gifted and thoroughly prepared labor force is a critical resource of the German monetary model. The country's accentuation on professional schooling and preparing is eminent. The "double framework" of professional preparation joins homeroom guidance with viable, hands on experience, getting ready youthful grown-ups for vocations in different ventures.

The German apprenticeship framework cultivates serious areas of strength for an among managers and instructive organizations, guaranteeing that the labor force is furnished with the abilities that address the issues of the gig market. This obligation to professional preparation has been instrumental in creating a labor force prestigious for its specialized skill and flexibility.

Advancement and Exploration:

Germany has reliably put resources into innovative work (Research and development), cultivating advancement across businesses. The nation's examination organizations and colleges keep areas of strength for an on science and innovation. In addition, the Fraunhofer Society, Europe's biggest application-situated research association, teams up intimately with organizations to drive mechanical progressions and address complex designing difficulties.

The idea of "Industry 4.0," which advocates for the combination of advanced advances into assembling processes, has gotten some decent momentum in Germany. It advances the utilization of computerization, information trade, and man-made consciousness to upgrade fabricating effectiveness and efficiency, situating Germany as a forerunner in modern robotization and the use of shrewd advances.

Social Wellbeing Net and Work Relations:

The German financial model puts major areas of strength for an on the government assistance of its residents. It flaunts a complete social security net that incorporates all inclusive medical care, joblessness advantages, and admittance to quality instruction. The social market economy means to adjust the quest for benefit with the insurance of individual prosperity.

The German work market includes an arrangement of "co-assurance," which guarantees that specialists have something to do with corporate dynamic through the presence of work delegates on organization sheets. This framework cultivates collaboration among work and the board and empowers a steady and useful work space. Worker's guilds and business affiliations assume huge parts in forming work relations and guaranteeing fair wages and working circumstances.

Send out Drove Development and Exchange Overflows:

Germany's commodity driven economy is a sign of its prosperity. The nation reliably keeps up with exchange overflows, sending out labor and products all over the planet. The strength of the German assembling area, the nature of its items, and its obligation to development make it a worldwide forerunner in global exchange.

The "Mittelstand" assumes a urgent part in trading German-made products. These SMEs have a worldwide reach, giving specific items and administrations to global business sectors. Germany's commodity direction has contributed fundamentally to its financial security and development.

Monetary Difficulties and Changes:

Notwithstanding its momentous accomplishments, the German financial model faces a few difficulties. One key concern is segment change, described by a maturing populace and a low rate of birth. These elements have brought up issues about the maintainability of the social government assistance framework and the accessibility of a talented workforce.

In addition, the model's dependence on sends out has made the German economy helpless to worldwide monetary vacillations. Exchange pressures, changes in worldwide stock chains, and monetary emergencies can fundamentally affect Germany's financial presentation.

Contemporary Importance:

The German monetary model remaining parts profoundly important in the contemporary worldwide financial scene. Germany's obligation to assembling greatness and development, its gifted labor force, and its professional schooling system keep on being wellsprings of solidarity. The country's commitment to maintainability, exploration, and improvement guarantees its place at the cutting edge of mechanical progressions.

The model's accentuation on friendly government assistance and work relations has additionally set a model for different nations. The idea of offsetting financial accomplishment with social value has become progressively significant in conversations about mindful private enterprise.

Difficulties and Transformation:

To support its monetary achievement, Germany should address a few squeezing difficulties. Segment change requires imaginative answers for secure a talented labor force. Changes to the school system and the work market, as well as the mix of travelers and outcasts into the labor force, are regions that need consideration.

Germany's reliance on sends out requires progressing variation to changing worldwide exchange elements. Broadening of business sectors, more noteworthy interest in digitalization, and the improvement of homegrown interest can upgrade monetary strength.

The reception of computerized advancements and Industry 4.0 standards is one more road for development and change. German organizations should keep on embracing robotization, information examination, and computerized reasoning to stay serious in the worldwide market.

Maintainability and Ecological Obligation:

Germany's obligation to natural supportability and the green economy is acquiring conspicuousness. The nation has set aggressive focuses for decreasing ozone harming substance discharges and extending sustainable power sources. Drives, for example, the "Energiewende" (energy change) show Germany's commitment to tending to ecological difficulties while driving advancement and occupation creation in the sustainable power area.

Germany's designing and assembling skill assume a pivotal part in the improvement of clean advances, like breeze turbines and sunlight powered chargers. The nation's involvement with economical designing has situated it as a worldwide forerunner in the change to additional naturally capable modern practices.

5.2 Emphasis on precision engineering and manufacturing

Accuracy designing and assembling are at the center of present day modern achievement. The capacity to configuration, produce, and gather items with remarkable exactness, quality, and effectiveness is a principal driver of financial development and mechanical advancement. This account investigates the significance of accuracy designing and assembling, its authentic development, and its contemporary pertinence in different ventures.

Verifiable Establishments:

The underlying foundations of accuracy designing can be followed back to the beginning of the Modern Transformation when the interest for exchangeable parts prompted propels in assembling processes. Advancements like the machine and the micrometer were instrumental in accomplishing more prominent accuracy in metalworking. Subsequently, items turned out to be more solid, repairable, and financially savvy.

The idea of accuracy designing acquired conspicuousness during The Second Great War while the assembling of mind boggling military gear required exceptionally precise parts. The conflict exertion drove progressions in machining strategies, metrology (the study of estimation), and quality control techniques. These advancements laid the foundation for the post-war accuracy designing industry.

The Job of Accuracy Designing:

Accuracy designing is a multidisciplinary field that consolidates mechanical designing, optics, hardware, and materials science. It envelops the plan and creation of exact and complex parts utilized in different ventures, from aviation and clinical gadgets to car and buyer hardware. The quest for accuracy is driven by the requirement for items that meet severe exhibition prerequisites, whether it's a heart valve, a fly motor part, or a cell phone.

Accuracy designing is fundamental in making perplexing and sensitive gadgets, for example, microelectromechanical frameworks (MEMS), which are utilized in sensors, accelerometers, and clinical inserts. It likewise assumes a critical part in the improvement of nanotechnology, where accuracy at the nuclear and sub-atomic level is essential for making new materials and gadgets.

Producing Greatness:

Accuracy designing remains inseparable with assembling greatness. The quality and consistency of the assembling system are fundamental in accomplishing accuracy in the eventual outcome. Producing greatness depends on a mix of variables, including:

Progressed Machining Strategies: The utilization of cutting edge machining processes, like PC mathematical control (CNC) machining, electrical release machining (EDM), and laser cutting, empowers the creation of exceptionally exact parts. CNC machines, specifically, have changed the assembling business by offering high accuracy and robotization.

Resistances and Quality Control: Exact estimations and resiliences are characterized for every part, guaranteeing that they meet explicit models. Quality control measures, including non-disastrous testing and assessments, are executed to confirm consistence.

Material Determination: The selection of materials with the right properties, like hardness, strength, and warm conductivity, is critical in accuracy producing. Materials should be appropriate for the expected application.

Metrology and Estimation Instruments: Metrology assumes a focal part in accuracy designing, with instruments, for example, coordinate estimating machines (CMMs), optical estimation gadgets, and laser interferometers used to check the exactness of parts.

Uses of Accuracy Designing:

Accuracy designing significantly affects different businesses, driving advancement and empowering the improvement of state of the art items and innovations.

Aviation and Protection: The aeronautic trade requests the most elevated levels of accuracy in the plan and assembling of airplane, space apparatus, and safeguard hardware. Parts should meet severe resiliences to guarantee security and unwavering quality. Accuracy designing is basic for the improvement of cutting edge route frameworks, turbine sharp edges, and aeronautics.

Clinical Gadgets: Accuracy designing assumes a crucial part in the clinical field, from demonstrative gear to careful instruments and implantable gadgets. Inserts, like fake joints and heart pacemakers, depend on exact designing to work really inside the human body.

Buyer Gadgets: The scaling down of electronic parts and the improvement of high-goal presentations and sensors are made conceivable by accuracy designing. Cell phones, workstations, and wearables rely upon microengineering for their smaller and proficient plans.

Car Industry: Accuracy designing is fundamental for guaranteeing the unwavering quality and wellbeing of vehicles. High level assembling methods and exact machining are utilized to deliver motor parts, transmission parts, and elite execution brakes.

Optics and Photonics: Accuracy designing is principal to the advancement of optical frameworks, lasers, and imaging innovations. These parts are utilized in different applications, from broadcast communications to clinical imaging and logical exploration.

Semiconductor Industry: Accuracy designing is at the center of semiconductor producing, where nanoscale highlights should be made on silicon wafers with outrageous precision. The creation of computer chips, semiconductors, and incorporated circuits depends on cutting edge accuracy methods.

Energy Area: Accuracy designing adds to the improvement of energy-productive innovations, including wind turbines, sun powered chargers, and high level battery frameworks. These advancements are fundamental for tending to energy challenges and natural worries.

Challenges in Accuracy Designing:

While accuracy designing offers various advantages, it likewise presents difficulties that should be defeated to accomplish the ideal degree of exactness and quality.

Intricacy: Accuracy designing frequently includes many-sided and complex plans, which require progressed producing abilities and profoundly talented staff.

Material Determination: Picking the right materials with the ideal properties is urgent. Material attributes can fundamentally influence the accuracy of the finished result.

Resistance and Consistency: Keeping up with tight resiliences and consistency all through the creation cycle can challenge. Varieties in material properties, temperature, and ecological circumstances should be painstakingly controlled.

Quality Control: Guaranteeing that every part satisfies the pre-defined quality guidelines and resiliences requires thorough quality control measures and assessment processes.

Cost: Accomplishing high accuracy can be exorbitant, as it might include specific hardware, talented work, and fastidious quality confirmation.

Contemporary Pertinence:

In the computerized age, accuracy designing has acquired much more importance. The interest for more modest, quicker, and more proficient items has prompted progressions in miniature and nano-technology, which depend vigorously on accuracy designing. This is apparent in the improvement of nanoscale semiconductors for micro processors, profoundly exact sensors for independent vehicles, and scaled down clinical gadgets.

Besides, accuracy designing is key to the Fourth Modern Upheaval, frequently alluded to as Industry 4.0. The coordination of computerized advances, like the Web of Things (IoT), man-made consciousness, and computerization, into assembling processes is changing accuracy designing. Brilliant processing plants and computerized twin innovations are upgrading accuracy and effectiveness, while information examination give constant bits of knowledge to quality control.

Natural Obligation and Supportability:

As accuracy designing keeps on developing, there is a developing spotlight on natural obligation and supportability. The development of high-accuracy parts can be asset serious, and the removal of waste materials and synthetic compounds should be overseen capably.

Maintainable designing practices plan to limit squander, diminish energy utilization, and utilize harmless to the ecosystem materials. For instance, the airplane business is investigating lightweight, eco-accommodating materials to further develop eco-friendliness, while the auto business is moving toward electric vehicles to diminish outflows. These drives line up with worldwide endeavors to address environmental change and advance supportable assembling.

5.3 Sustainability and the role of the Mittelstand

Supportability has arisen as a focal subject in present day monetary and modern conversations. It incorporates a promise to ecological insurance, dependable asset the board, and an emphasis on long haul monetary feasibility. Inside the German financial scene, the Mittelstand, an assortment of little and medium-sized ventures (SMEs), assumes a significant part in supporting maintainability. This account investigates the idea of supportability and the critical commitments of the Mittelstand in such manner.

Figuring out Maintainability:

Maintainability is a multi-layered idea that goes past natural worries. It epitomizes three key aspects: natural maintainability, social manageability, and monetary supportability. These aspects are frequently alluded to as the "triple primary concern."

Ecological Manageability: This aspect centers around the preservation of normal assets, the decrease of natural effect, and the advancement of perfect and environmentally friendly power sources. Natural manageability underscores dependable asset the executives and the moderation of environmental change.

Social Maintainability: Social supportability relates to the prosperity of people, networks, and social orders all in all. It includes fair work rehearses, local area commitment, variety and incorporation, and the security of basic freedoms.

Financial Supportability: Monetary maintainability includes guaranteeing the drawn out reasonability of monetary frameworks. This incorporates monetary soundness, financial development, and a promise to moral strategic policies that forestall extortion, debasement, and double-dealing.

The quest for manageability looks to adjust these three aspects, making an amicable and prosperous society while safeguarding the climate and guaranteeing financial strength. This all encompassing methodology perceives that monetary advancement should not come to the detriment of social and ecological prosperity.

The Job of the Mittelstand:

The Mittelstand is an interesting element of the German monetary scene. Containing more than the vast majority of all organizations in Germany, these little and medium-sized undertakings are the foundation of the nation's economy. They are known for their flexibility, advancement, and obligation to quality, and they fundamentally add to business and financial development.

The Mittelstand is much of the time family-possessed and centers around particular, specialty markets. While they may not be all around as extensive as worldwide organizations, their aggregate impact is significant. As far as manageability, the Mittelstand assumes an essential part in more than one way.

Development and Exploration: Numerous Mittelstand organizations are pioneers in specialty showcases and have a profound comprehension of their businesses. This positions them to foster imaginative arrangements that are many times more light-footed and receptive to changing supportability requests. These organizations take part in innovative work, zeroing in on green advancements and feasible practices.

Asset Proficiency: Maintainability is firmly connected to asset productivity. Mittelstand firms frequently succeed in upgrading their cycles and utilizing assets successfully. Their capacity to accomplish more with less diminishes squander, limits energy utilization, and limits natural effect.

Neighborhood and Provincial Concentration: The Mittelstand frequently has solid nearby and territorial ties. This makes them more delicate to the prosperity of the networks where they work. They effectively draw in with nearby partners, add to local area advancement, and backing social and natural drives in their areas.

Stable Business: The Mittelstand values its workers and will in general give steady, long haul business. This approach is lined up with the standards of social manageability, guaranteeing that specialists get fair wages and professional stability.

Better standards without ever compromising: Mittelstand firms focus on higher standards when in doubt, guaranteeing that their items and administrations fulfill high guidelines. This obligation to quality frequently reaches out to manageable practices, as all things considered, very much fabricated items will have a more drawn out life expectancy and diminished ecological effect.

Flexibility: Mittelstand organizations are known for their versatility and responsiveness to advertise changes. This trademark positions them to rapidly incorporate supportable practices into their activities and foster items that line up with arising supportability patterns.

Consolidating Maintainability in Mittelstand Practices:

The Mittelstand's obligation to supportability is apparent through different practices and drives that line up with the triple primary concern of ecological, social, and financial maintainability.

Energy Proficiency: Numerous Mittelstand organizations put resources into energy-productive innovations and practices. They take on energy-productive lighting, central air frameworks, and assembling cycles to lessen energy utilization and ozone depleting substance emanations. They frequently take part in drives like energy reviews and the execution of environmentally friendly power sources.

Squander Decrease: Supportability cognizant Mittelstand firms center around lessening waste by upgrading creation processes, reusing materials, and limiting superfluous bundling. These practices save costs as well as add to ecological maintainability.

Practical Inventory Chains: Mittelstand organizations are progressively considering the maintainability of their stock chains. They source materials and parts from providers who stick to capable and moral works on, advancing social supportability.

Local area Commitment: The Mittelstand frequently assumes a huge part in their nearby networks. They support nearby causes, take part in instructive drives, and effectively take part in local area projects that advance social prosperity.

Advancement in Green Advancements: Mittelstand firms are at the cutting edge of creating and taking on green advancements. Whether it's in sustainable power, feasible farming, or productive assembling processes, they add to natural maintainability through their advancement endeavors.

Representative Prosperity: Numerous Mittelstand organizations focus on the prosperity of their workers. They give preparing and proficient improvement open doors, offer adaptable working game plans, and advance balance between serious and fun activities, adding to social maintainability.

Client Driven Approach: Mittelstand firms frequently focus on their clients' manageability objectives. They work intimately with their clients to furnish items and administrations that line up with manageability norms and inclinations.

Difficulties and Open doors:

While the Mittelstand is effectively participated in maintainability rehearses, it faces its own arrangement of difficulties and open doors in chasing after supportable turn of events.

Monetary Limitations: More modest undertakings might have restricted monetary assets to put resources into manageability drives, making it trying to execute costly green advancements or participate in enormous scope ecological ventures.

Admittance to Data: More modest organizations might have restricted admittance to data and assets connected with supportability. They might require backing and direction to explore complex maintainability norms and guidelines.

Administrative Consistence: Staying aware of advancing maintainability guidelines and norms can be trying for SMEs. They need to remain educated and consistent to meet legitimate prerequisites and market assumptions.

Inventory network Supportability: Keeping up with maintainability principles across the whole inventory network, including providers and subcontractors, can be mind boggling. Guaranteeing that each accomplice sticks to capable and moral practices presents a huge test.

Market Access: The capacity to get to worldwide business sectors relies upon meeting different maintainability prerequisites and affirmations. SMEs should comprehend and satisfy these standards to grow their compass.

Worldwide Importance of Mittelstand Supportability:

The maintainability endeavors of the Mittelstand resound past Germany's boundaries. As maintainability turns into a worldwide concern, organizations overall are hoping to take on naturally and socially capable practices. Mittelstand firms offer significant bits of knowledge and instances of how to effectively adjust financial development, social prosperity, and natural obligation.

In addition, Mittelstand firms frequently work together with worldwide accomplices, and their manageability drives can impact worldwide stockpile chains. By taking on and advancing maintainability rehearses, they add to worldwide supportability endeavors and assist with forming global principles.

6

Chapter 6

South Korea: Innovation and Exports

South Korea has arisen as a worldwide force to be reckoned with in development and products in the 21st hundred years. This surprising change can be credited to a blend of variables, including areas of strength for a to training, an emphasis on innovative work, and a unique business climate. South Korea's excursion from a conflict torn country to a monetary and innovative goliath is a demonstration of the country's strength and assurance.

One of the vital drivers of South Korea's progress in development and products is its school system. The nation puts areas of strength for on instruction since the beginning, with an exceptionally serious and thorough tutoring framework. South Korean understudies reliably rank among the top entertainers in global evaluations, and the nation brags one the most noteworthy proficiency rates on the planet. This obligation to training has created a profoundly gifted and instructed labor force, which is fundamental for development and product drove development.

Notwithstanding a solid instructive establishment, South Korea has put vigorously in innovative work (Research and development). The public authority plays had a critical impact in supporting Research and development exercises through different drives and subsidizing programs. South Korea's Research and development spending as a level of Gross domestic product is among the most elevated on the planet, and this venture has prompted pivotal developments in different businesses, from gadgets and auto to biotechnology and mechanical technology. Organizations like Samsung, LG, and Hyundai have become worldwide forerunners in their particular areas, on account of their obligation to Research and development.

Moreover, South Korea has developed a powerful business climate that cultivates development and business. The public authority has executed strategies to advance startup culture and funding speculation. These drives have prompted the rise of various fruitful tech new companies in fields like web based business, fintech, and man-made reasoning. South Korea's tech biological system is energetic, with bunches of development focuses and research establishments that team up with organizations to drive progress.

The country's development culture is well established in its Confucian legacy, which esteems difficult work, discipline, and persistent personal growth. This social outlook, joined with the cutting edge foundation and admittance to worldwide business sectors, has made South Korea a development center with a worldwide reach. The Korean Wave, or "Hallyu," which alludes to the worldwide prominence of South Korean music, motion pictures, and TV dramatizations, is a demonstration of the country's capacity to make and commodity social items.

South Korea's progress in advancement and commodities is additionally intently attached to its exchange approaches and global organizations. The nation has reliably sought after an open and commodity situated procedure, which has permitted it to flourish in the worldwide commercial center. South Korea is known for its international alliances with significant economies, like the US, European Association, and ASEAN nations. These arrangements have worked with exchange and market access, empowering South Korean items to arrive at customers around the world.

One of South Korea's most huge accomplishments has been in the hardware business. The ascent of organizations like Samsung and LG Hardware has made South Korea a worldwide forerunner in customer gadgets, semiconductor assembling, and show innovation. These organizations have reliably pushed the limits of advancement, creating state of the art items that are sought after around the world. South Korea's hardware trades play had a crucial impact in the country's monetary development and worldwide seriousness.

The auto business is another area where South Korea has taken significant steps. Organizations like Hyundai, Kia, and Beginning have earned respect for delivering excellent vehicles that are famous locally as well as in worldwide business sectors. Their obligation to development and mechanical progressions has made South Korean vehicles serious on a worldwide scale. The progress of South Korean automakers exhibits the country's capacity to succeed in conventional businesses while embracing new advancements.

Biotechnology and medical care have additionally become areas of concentration for South Korea. The nation has put vigorously in biotechnology research, prompting headways in clinical medicines and drugs. South Korean biotech firms are associated with state of the art research, and their items are popular globally. The worldwide Coronavirus pandemic featured South Korea's abilities in testing, contact following, and immunization creation, further laying out its standing in the biotechnology area.

South Korea's progress in development and products isn't restricted to the tech and car ventures. The nation is additionally known for its shipbuilding, steel, and petrochemical areas, which contribute fundamentally to its all products and financial development. South Korean combinations, known as "chaebols," assume a critical part in these businesses and are instrumental in extending the country's worldwide impression.

As of late, South Korea has gained significant headway in the environmentally friendly power area. The public authority has been effectively advancing green advancements and putting resources into environmentally friendly power sources, for example, sunlight based and wind power. This obligation to supportability lines up with worldwide endeavors to battle environmental change and can possibly set out new product open doors for South Korean organizations spend significant time in green advances.

South Korea's worldwide reach stretches out to the diversion and social businesses. The Korean Wave, or Hallyu, has cleared across the world, with K-popular music, Korean shows, and Korean cooking acquiring monstrous prevalence. This social peculiarity has not just reinforced South Korea's commodities of diversion items yet has likewise prompted expanded the travel industry and a developing interest in South Korean language and culture.

With regards to worldwide exchange, South Korea is a basic player. The nation's product driven economy is exceptionally subject to global business sectors. While this has brought gigantic thriving, it has likewise presented South Korea to outer financial shocks and worldwide vulnerabilities. For instance, exchange pressures and protectionist strategies different nations can influence South Korean products. The nation should explore these difficulties while proceeding to cultivate development and innovative headway.

One of the continuous difficulties for South Korea is its relationship with North Korea. The Korean Landmass stays partitioned, with the neutral ground (DMZ) filling in as an actual sign of this division. Political strains and the potential for struggle with North Korea have forever been a worry for South Korea, influencing the solidness and security of the locale. Notwithstanding, the South Korean government has reliably sought after strategic endeavors to ease pressures and work towards a quiet reunification of the Korean Landmass.

South Korea's development and commodity achievement isn't without its inward difficulties too. In spite of the country's noteworthy monetary development, it wrestles with issues connected with pay imbalance and an exceptionally serious schooling system that puts monstrous strain on understudies. The public authority keeps on dealing with strategies pointed toward resolving these social and monetary issues, endeavoring to make a more comprehensive and fair society.

South Korea's development and commodity ability have not slipped through the cracks on the worldwide stage. The nation is effectively engaged with global associations, like the Assembled Countries and the World Exchange Association. It additionally takes part in different provincial discussions and drives, including the Asia-Pacific Monetary Collaboration (APEC) and the Relationship of Southeast Asian Countries (ASEAN). South Korea's commitments to these associations mirror its obligation to worldwide soundness, financial turn of events, and exchange collaboration.

The eventual fate of South Korea's development and product potential is promising, yet it isn't without its difficulties. One of the vital drivers of South Korea's prosperity is its capacity to adjust to changing worldwide elements. The world is encountering quick innovative progressions, including the ascent of man-made reasoning, the web of things, and the fourth modern transformation. South Korea should keep on putting resources into these arising advances to keep up with its strategic advantage in the worldwide market.

South Korea additionally faces contest from other arising economies, especially in Asia. Nations like China and India have quickly extending economies and are progressively putting resources into advancement and innovation. South Korea should stay watchful and proactive in remaining ahead in regions like high level assembling, computerized advances, and man-made reasoning.

Besides, South Korea's populace is maturing quickly, which presents segment difficulties. The nation needs to resolve issues connected with a maturing labor force, government backed retirement, and medical services to guarantee that it can support monetary development and advancement in the long haul.

The worldwide financial scene is ceaselessly developing, and South Korea's capacity to adjust and improve will be fundamental for its proceeded with progress. It should offset monetary development with ecological manageability and social value to guarantee a prosperous and stable future.

All in all, South Korea's noteworthy excursion from a conflict torn country to a monetary and mechanical force to be reckoned with is a demonstration of its obligation to training, development, and commodities. The country's solid schooling system, interest in innovative work, and dynamic business climate have impelled it to worldwide noticeable quality. South Korea's progress in gadgets, car, biotechnology, and social products has made it a key part in the worldwide economy.

6.1 South Korea's rapid economic growth

South Korea's quick monetary development throughout the course of recent many years is completely striking. The nation has changed from a conflict torn country during the 1950s to one of the world's driving economies in the 21st hundred years. This change can be credited to a blend of elements, including vital government strategies, a solid obligation to schooling, an emphasis on industrialization, and a unique product situated approach. South Korea's development story fills in as a significant contextual investigation being developed financial matters and offers significant examples for different nations taking a stab at monetary flourishing.

South Korea's post-war period was set apart by decimation, as the Korean Conflict (1950-1953) left the nation in ruins. The monetary scene was critical, with elevated degrees of neediness, little industrialization, and restricted framework. Notwithstanding, in the years that followed, South Korea left on an excursion of fast financial development and improvement.

One of the vital drivers of South Korea's monetary development was its administration's obligation to key preparation and intercession. The nation embraced a progression of five-year plans, enlivened by the Soviet Association's model, to direct its financial turn of events. These plans set explicit focuses for different areas of the economy, like assembling, foundation, and training, and intended to activate assets toward accomplishing these objectives.

The South Korean government assumed a focal part in directing the country's monetary development. It offered monetary help to designated enterprises, offered motivators for speculation, and empowered the improvement of basic foundation. Furthermore, it executed a strategy of commodity drove development, perceiving the significance of global business sectors for its monetary extension.

The obligation to schooling was one more essential figure South Korea's development story. The public authority put vigorously in building areas of strength for a framework, stressing general admittance to training, excellent schools, and an emphasis on science and innovation. This interest in human resources made a profoundly gifted labor force that would later drive the nation's industrialization and development.

South Korea likewise took on areas of strength for an on industrialization as a vital driver of monetary development. The public authority distinguished key enterprises that had the potential for development and offered help and motivations to advance their turn of events. This methodology, frequently alluded to as "modern strategy," was instrumental in the outcome of enterprises like steel, shipbuilding, and gadgets.

The "Supernatural occurrence on the Han Waterway" is a term frequently used to portray South Korea's quick industrialization and monetary development. The Han Stream goes through Seoul, South Korea's capital, and its change from a generally lacking country to a modern force to be reckoned with was to be sure supernatural. South Korea's industrialization was portrayed by a shift from an agrarian culture to one driven by assembling and innovation.

The weighty and substance ventures assumed an essential part in South Korea's industrialization. The public authority offered monetary help and motivators to advance the development of these areas.

Organizations like POSCO (Pohang Iron and Steel Organization) and Hyundai Weighty Ventures arose as pioneers in their particular enterprises, driving critical financial development.

The Korean government likewise assumed an essential part in sustaining its early vehicle industry. Hyundai, Kia, and Daewoo (presently a piece of General Engines) entered the worldwide market, creating reasonable and excellent vehicles that acquired fame both locally and globally. The progress of South Korean automakers exhibited the country's capacity to contend in a profoundly serious worldwide industry.

Gadgets is another area where South Korea has made colossal progress. Organizations like Samsung and LG have become worldwide monsters in buyer gadgets, semiconductor assembling, and show innovation. Their obligation to innovative work has prompted state of the art developments, and their items are popular around the world. The gadgets business has been a significant supporter of South Korea's monetary development.

South Korea's commodity situated approach was instrumental in its financial development. The nation perceived the significance of worldwide business sectors for its items and effectively looked to extend its worldwide reach. The public authority arranged economic accords with significant economies and urged South Korean organizations to enter global business sectors. This commodity driven system assisted the country with producing critical unfamiliar trade income and make occupations.

The Asian monetary emergency of 1997 essentially affected South Korea's economy. The emergency uncovered weaknesses in the country's monetary framework and prompted a sharp financial constriction. In any case, South Korea answered with a progression of financial changes and rebuilding endeavors that balanced out the economy and set it back on a development direction. The emergency filled in as an opportunity for growth and built up the requirement for a tough and enhanced economy.

South Korea's outcome in monetary development isn't exclusively ascribed to the public authority's arrangements and modern methodologies. The country's dynamic business climate and enterprising soul play had a fundamental influence. The "chaebols," enormous family-claimed aggregates, have been instrumental in driving monetary development. Organizations like Samsung, Hyundai, and LG have reliably adjusted to changing worldwide business sectors, put resources into innovative work, and extended their item portfolios.

Besides, South Korea's social commodities have turned into a critical piece of its worldwide presence. The Korean Wave, or "Hallyu," alludes to the worldwide prominence of South Korean music, films, TV shows, and cooking. This social peculiarity has not just supported South Korea's commodities of amusement items however has additionally expanded the travel industry and created worldwide interest in Korean language and culture.

Notwithstanding its momentous accomplishments, South Korea has confronted difficulties and weaknesses on its way to financial development. One of the continuous difficulties is the requirement for monetary broadening. The nation has been intensely dependent on a couple of key enterprises, like hardware and cars. To guarantee reasonable development, South Korea should keep on broadening its economy and put resources into arising areas, including environmentally friendly power, biotechnology, and man-made brainpower.

South Korea's populace is likewise maturing quickly, introducing segment difficulties. The nation needs to resolve issues connected with a maturing labor force, government managed retirement, and medical services to guarantee that it can support financial development and keep up with its exclusive requirement of living.

The worldwide monetary scene is consistently developing, with new mechanical progressions and changes in worldwide exchange elements. South Korea should keep on adjusting to these progressions and put resources into arising advancements to stay serious in the worldwide market. The ascent of computerized reasoning, computerization, and the fourth modern upset presents the two open doors and difficulties that South Korea should explore.

South Korea's relationship with North Korea stays an intricate and irritating issue. The Korean Promontory stays partitioned, with political pressures and the potential for struggle. South Korea's craving for harmony and reunification presents the two difficulties and potential open doors for its monetary development and security.

All in all, South Korea's fast financial development is a demonstration of its essential government strategies, solid obligation to schooling, center around industrialization, and dynamic product situated approach. The nation's excursion from present conflict pulverization on a worldwide financial stalwart fills in as a rousing example of overcoming adversity in the domain of improvement financial matters.

South Korea's "Wonder on the Han Stream" was portrayed by its change from an agrarian culture to a modern and mechanical force to be reckoned with. The public authority's contribution in designated modern strategies, joined with areas of strength for an on human resources improvement, pushed the nation's development. Ventures like steel, shipbuilding, gadgets, and vehicles became worldwide pioneers, contributing fundamentally to the country's financial achievement.

South Korea's product driven approach, with a guarantee to worldwide exchange and the discussion of economic deals, assumed a significant part in its development. The country's dynamic business climate and pioneering soul, addressed by the chaebols, have additionally been instrumental in its accomplishments.

Social products, especially the Korean Wave, have added to South Korea's worldwide presence, prompting expanded the travel industry and worldwide interest in Korean culture. While South Korea has confronted difficulties connected with monetary expansion, a maturing populace, and the need to adjust to new advances, its strength and flexibility stay integral to its proceeded with progress.

The worldwide financial scene is always developing, and South Korea's capacity to adjust to new advances and explore international difficulties will be fundamental for its future development. The country's obligation to development, broadening, and supportability will decide its capacity to keep up with its situation as a main worldwide economy. South Korea's wonderful monetary development venture remains as a demonstration of what a country can accomplish with vital preparation, an emphasis on schooling, and an assurance to succeed.

6.2 Focus on innovation and technology

In the cutting edge period, development and innovation have become focal drivers of monetary development, flourishing, and worldwide seriousness. Countries that focus on development and put resources into innovation improvement frequently wind up at the front of financial headways. South Korea is a great representation of a country that has outfit the force of development and innovation to accomplish striking development and worldwide noticeable quality.

South Korea's obligation to advancement and innovation can be followed back to its post-war remaking endeavors during the twentieth hundred years. Perceiving the need to reconstruct its crushed economy, the South Korean government pursued an essential choice to focus on instruction and the improvement of an exceptionally talented labor force. Schooling turned into a foundation of South Korea's development procedure, establishing the groundwork for its innovative progressions.

One of the most prominent parts of South Korea's schooling system is its accentuation on science, innovation, designing, and arithmetic (STEM) fields. The nation puts extraordinary significance on STEM training, empowering understudies to succeed in these disciplines since the beginning. This emphasis on STEM has brought about South Korean understudies reliably positioning among the top entertainers in global evaluations, delivering an ability pool that is exceptional to drive mechanical headways.

South Korea's commitment to instruction stretches out to advanced education foundations also. The nation flaunts renowned colleges and examination focuses that direct state of the art research in different fields. These foundations act as centers for advancement and innovation improvement, cultivating coordinated effort among the scholarly world and industry.

The public authority plays had a critical impact in supporting innovative work (Research and development) exercises in South Korea. The obligation to Research and development is obvious in the nation's elevated degrees of interest around here. South Korea reliably distributes a significant piece of its Gross domestic product to Research and development, making it one of the world's driving nations as far as Research and development spending.

The effect of this venture should be visible across different enterprises. South Korean organizations are at the cutting edge of advancement in areas like gadgets, biotechnology, car, and semiconductors. Remarkably, South Korea is home to worldwide tech monsters like Samsung and LG Hardware, which have made critical commitments to the improvement of purchaser gadgets, semiconductor assembling, and show innovation.

Quite possibly of the most extraordinary mechanical headway that South Korea has accomplished is the far reaching reception of 5G innovation. The nation was among quick to carry out 5G organizations, which offer fundamentally quicker web velocities and lower idleness. This mechanical jump has prepared for different applications, from expanded reality to the Web of Things (IoT), and has situated South Korea as a forerunner in the worldwide broadcast communications industry.

South Korea's car industry is another area that has profited from development and innovation. Organizations like Hyundai, Kia, and Beginning have zeroed in on creating electric and independent vehicles, mirroring the worldwide shift toward economical and savvy portability arrangements. Their interests in Research and development and development have empowered South Korean automakers to contend on a worldwide scale.

Biotechnology is one more region where South Korea has taken wonderful steps. The country's biotech firms are engaged with momentous exploration in fields like genomics, drugs, and regenerative medication. South Korea's biotechnology area assumed a critical part in the battle against the Coronavirus pandemic, with the nation quickly creating demonstrative tests and adding to immunization exploration and creation.

The public authority's contribution in development and innovation goes past financing. South Korea has executed strategies to help new businesses and cultivate a culture of business. These drives have prompted the development of various fruitful tech new businesses in fields like online business, fintech, and man-made consciousness. South Korea's tech biological system is dynamic, with bunches of development focuses and research organizations that team up with organizations to drive progress.

South Korea's advancement culture is well established in its Confucian legacy, which esteems difficult work, discipline, and consistent personal development. This social outlook, joined with current framework and admittance to worldwide business sectors, has made South Korea a development center with a worldwide reach. The nation's "can-do" soul and obligation to greatness have pushed it to the bleeding edge of the innovation and advancement scene.

One of the main parts of South Korea's innovation and advancement venture is its worldwide reach. The nation effectively sends out its innovative items and ability to business sectors all over the planet. South Korean organizations have laid down a good foundation for themselves as confided in worldwide accomplices, providing basic parts for many businesses, from cell phones and TVs to auto and aviation.

South Korea's mechanical ability is exemplified in its commodities of semiconductor items. The nation is a predominant player in the semiconductor business, with organizations like Samsung and SK Hynix being significant supporters of the worldwide stockpile of memory chips. These chips are basic parts in endless electronic gadgets, and South Korea's capacity to reliably enhance in this field has set its worldwide position.

The worldwide Coronavirus pandemic featured South Korea's mechanical and development capacities. The country's quick reaction, including broad testing, contact following, and the advancement of computerized devices to deal with the emergency, gathered global commendation. South Korea's capacity to use innovation for compelling pandemic control fills in as a model for different countries confronting comparative difficulties.

South Korea's obligation to manageability and natural obligation is one more part of its advancement and innovation endeavors. The nation has put resources into sustainable power sources, for example, sun based and wind power, planning to lessen its carbon impression and progress to a green economy. This attention on maintainability lines up with worldwide endeavors to battle environmental change and presents new open doors for South Korean organizations spend significant time in green advancements.

In the domain of room investigation, South Korea has gained critical headway. The nation sent off its most memorable space traveler, Yi So-yeon, into space in 2008, and it has since kept on putting resources into space exploration and satellite innovation. South Korea's space program addresses its goals to add to the worldwide space local area and tackle the advantages of room related innovations.

South Korea's attention on development and innovation isn't restricted to customary enterprises. The country's computerized change and interests in man-made brainpower (simulated intelligence) have been picking up speed. South Korea perceives the capability of man-made intelligence to drive financial development and work on different parts of society, from medical care and training to transportation and shrewd urban communities.

While South Korea's accomplishments in advancement and innovation are significant, the nation isn't without its difficulties. The fast speed of mechanical change and worldwide contest require steady transformation. South Korea should keep on putting resources into innovative work, especially in arising regions like artificial intelligence and biotechnology, to remain ahead in the worldwide race for mechanical administration.

Besides, South Korea's populace is maturing quickly, presenting segment difficulties. The nation should resolve issues connected with a maturing labor force, government backed retirement, and medical care to guarantee that it can support its financial development and mechanical headways.

South Korea's progress in advancement and innovation has additionally been joined by worries connected with protection and information security. As the nation embraces new computerized innovations, it should adjust the advantages of mechanical progressions with defending people's protection and getting touchy information.

The worldwide financial scene is consistently developing, with new difficulties and amazing open doors arising. South Korea's capacity to adjust to these progressions and keep encouraging development and mechanical headway will be fundamental for its future development and intensity. The ascent of man-made consciousness, robotization, and the fourth modern insurgency presents the two potential open doors and difficulties that South Korea should explore.

All in all, South Korea's emphasis on development and innovation has been vital to its exceptional monetary development and worldwide noticeable quality. The country's obligation to instruction, innovative work, and a unique business climate has pushed it to the front line of the worldwide innovation scene.

South Korea's accomplishments in fields like gadgets, auto, biotechnology, and semiconductors feature its advancement capacities. The country's interests in 5G innovation, electric and independent vehicles, and biotechnology have situated it as a forerunner in the worldwide field.

The public authority's approaches to help new companies and business have prompted the development of effective tech new businesses in different fields. South Korea's tech biological system, established in a culture of difficult work and greatness, keeps on driving development and coordinated effort among the scholarly world and industry.

South Korea's worldwide reach is a demonstration of its innovative mastery. The nation effectively sends out its mechanical items and administrations, and South Korean organizations have secured themselves as confided in worldwide accomplices in different enterprises. South Korea's capacity to enhance, adjust, and answer worldwide difficulties, as shown during the Coronavirus pandemic, builds up its situation as a worldwide innovation and development pioneer.

6.3 The importance of exports and conglomerates

Commodities and combinations assume a pivotal part in the financial turn of events and worldwide situating of countries. This entwined connection among products and combinations has been especially obvious on account of South Korea. As one of the world's driving product driven economies, South Korea's aggregates, frequently alluded to as "chaebols," have been instrumental in driving the nation's commodity achievement and adding to its monetary development and advancement.

South Korea's excursion to turning into a commodity arranged force to be reckoned with can be followed back to its post-war remaking period during the twentieth hundred years. Following the Korean Conflict, which left the country in ruins, South Korea confronted the overwhelming errand of modifying its economy. Without any significant regular assets, the public authority perceived that products would be fundamental for creating unfamiliar trade income and invigorating monetary development.

The South Korean government embraced a proactive way to deal with advancing products, laying out the Korea Exchange Advancement Enterprise (KOTRA) in 1962 to work with exchange and interface South Korean organizations with worldwide business sectors. This early spotlight on sends out set up for the country's future monetary achievement.

One of the key elements driving South Korea's commodity development has been its capacity to deliver superior grade, inventive, and cutthroat items. The combinations or chaebols, with their different business portfolios, have been vital in such manner. These business combinations are portrayed by their family-claimed structure, with huge control and impact over a large number of ventures and areas.

The chaebols play had a huge impact in driving South Korea's commodity achievement, with noticeable names like Samsung, Hyundai, LG, and SK Gathering driving the way. These combinations have wandered into different areas, from gadgets and cars to shipbuilding, steel, and petrochemicals, and have become prevailing players on the worldwide stage.

Gadgets is one of the most striking areas where South Korean aggregates have succeeded. Samsung, specifically, has accomplished worldwide acknowledgment for its development and market predominance. The organization's assorted item portfolio incorporates cell phones, TVs, semiconductors, and domestic devices. Samsung's mechanical progressions and item quality have made it a commonly recognized name overall and have essentially added to South Korea's commodity numbers.

The car business is another region where South Korean combinations have taken significant steps. Hyundai, Kia, and Beginning have secured themselves as worldwide contenders, creating excellent vehicles that are well known both locally and universally. The development and mechanical progressions of South Korean automakers have added to the nation's product achievement and worldwide monetary situating.

Notwithstanding gadgets and auto, the aggregates have made their presence felt in the shipbuilding business. Organizations like Hyundai Weighty Enterprises and Daewoo Shipbuilding and Marine Designing play had a fundamental impact in the worldwide sea area. These organizations have gotten global agreements for building huge, complex vessels and seaward stages, adding to South Korea's commodity ability in this industry.

The steel business is another area where South Korean aggregates have made critical commitments to the nation's products. POSCO (Pohang Iron and Steel Organization) is one of the world's driving steel makers, trading its top notch steel items to different nations. The organization's trend setting innovation and effective creation processes have given it an upper hand in the worldwide market.

The petrochemical area has additionally profited from the inclusion of combinations like LG and SK Gathering. These organizations are participated in the development of synthetics, plastics, and energy items, and their products have helped support South Korea's monetary development. The petrochemical business is profoundly aggressive, and South Korean aggregates' obligation to development and quality has permitted them to keep up with their worldwide piece of the pie.

South Korea's combinations are not restricted to customary ventures; they have ventured into arising areas, including sustainable power, biotechnology, and man-made reasoning. These enhancements mirror their flexibility and their acknowledgment of the significance of remaining at the front line of innovative headways.

As of late, South Korea has zeroed in on sustainable power and green advancements. The public authority has acquainted approaches with advance the turn of events and reception of sustainable power sources, for example, sun based and wind power. The aggregates have effectively partaken in this change, putting resources into clean energy activities and advances. The obligation to manageability lines up with worldwide endeavors to battle environmental change and opens up new commodity valuable open doors for South Korean organizations spend significant time in green advancements.

The biotechnology area is another region where South Korean aggregates have made huge speculations. The country's biotech firms are associated with state of the art research in genomics, drugs, and regenerative medication. Their developments and items have tracked down worldwide interest, particularly in the midst of the Coronavirus pandemic, where South Korea assumed a critical part in delivering symptomatic tests and adding to immunization examination and creation.

South Korea's aggregates have likewise wandered into the field of man-made brainpower (simulated intelligence). Simulated intelligence is perceived as a groundbreaking innovation with expansive applications, from mechanization and mechanical technology to medical services and money. South Korean aggregates are putting resources into simulated intelligence innovative work, trying to situate themselves as pioneers in this arising field.

The combinations have utilized their worldwide presence to send out a large number of items, from purchaser products and modern gear to foundation tasks and designing administrations. South Korean organizations have laid out worldwide organizations and supply chains, further reinforcing the nation's situation as a key part in the worldwide economy.

The combinations' worldwide reach stretches out past items to global consolidations and acquisitions. South Korean aggregates have procured unfamiliar organizations and shaped key associations to extend their worldwide presence and get close enough to new business sectors. This methodology has permitted them to expand their business portfolios and secure important resources around the world.

The Korean Wave, or "Hallyu," addresses South Korea's progress in sending out social items and diversion. K-popular music, Korean dramatizations, films, and food have acquired massive fame around the world. South Korean combinations play had a critical impact in advancing and circulating these social items universally, adding to the nation's delicate power and worldwide impact.

The combinations have likewise been effectively engaged with framework projects in far off nations. South Korean development and designing firms have gotten agreements for significant framework projects, including streets, extensions, rail routes, and power plants. These undertakings have supported South Korea's products as well as reinforced political and exchange relations with accomplice nations.

The connection among commodities and aggregates in South Korea isn't without its difficulties. One of the main pressing issues has been the convergence of financial influence and abundance inside these combinations, prompting issues connected with pay imbalance. The strength of the chaebols in different areas of the economy has brought up issues about fair rivalry and amazing open doors for more modest organizations.

The aggregates have confronted analysis for their mind boggling possession designs and issues of corporate administration. Endeavors have been made to improve straightforwardness and responsibility inside these combinations and address the difficulties of inordinate impact and control applied by the establishing families.

South Korea's aggregates have additionally needed to adjust to changing worldwide exchange elements and economic situations. Exchange pressures, protectionist strategies in different nations, and outer monetary shocks can affect South Korean commodities. The combinations should explore these difficulties while proceeding to cultivate development and mechanical progression.

Regardless of these difficulties, South Korea's aggregates stay essential to the country's monetary development and worldwide seriousness. They have been focal in driving South Korea's situation as a central part in global exchange, with an emphasis on development and the commodity of great items and administrations.

Chapter 7

Globalization and Trade

Globalization and exchange have been groundbreaking powers in the advanced world, forming economies, social orders, and worldwide relations. The course of globalization has advanced rapidly throughout recent many years, with exchange assuming a focal part interfacing nations, encouraging financial development, and advancing worldwide joining. This peculiarity has the two advantages and difficulties, and it is fundamental to comprehend the elements of globalization and exchange to explore the intricacies of our interconnected world.

Globalization, in wide terms, alludes to the rising interconnectedness and association of nations and social orders. It incorporates different perspectives, including monetary, political, social, and mechanical trades. Exchange is one of the most substantial and significant components of globalization, working with the trading of merchandise, administrations, and capital across borders.

One of the vital drivers of globalization has been propels in innovation and correspondence. The fast advancement of the web, media communications, and transportation frameworks has made it more straightforward for individuals, products, and thoughts to get across the world. These advances have decreased the boundaries to exchange and empowered nations to flawlessly partake in the worldwide economy more.

The course of globalization has not been uniform, and its effect shifts starting with one locale or country then onto the next. As far as some might be concerned, it has opened up new open doors for development and advancement, while for other people, it has presented critical difficulties. Understanding the different elements of globalization and exchange is fundamental for surveying the ramifications and molding approaches that can augment the advantages and limit the downsides.

Exchange is a crucial part of globalization, filling in as an impetus for monetary turn of events and worldwide collaboration. Nations take part in exchange for different reasons, including getting to assets, extending markets, and cultivating financial development. Exchange empowers specialization and the effective allotment of assets, as nations can zero in on delivering what they are generally aggressive in and trade these labor and products with others.

South Korea, for example, fills in as a magnificent illustration of a country that has utilized exchange to drive monetary development and improvement. The country's commodity situated approach, upheld by a solid obligation to instruction and development, has launch it from the vestiges of the Korean Conflict to becoming one of the world's driving economies.

South Korea's accentuation on exchange, joined with its dynamic combinations (chaebols) like Samsung and Hyundai, has been key to its financial achievement.

Worldwide exchange plays had a critical impact in South Korea's commodity driven economy. The nation perceived from the get-go that trading its items and administrations was pivotal for monetary development, especially without any bountiful normal assets. The public authority's proactive position in advancing commodities and the combinations' mechanical headways and advancement have permitted South Korean items to turn out to be around the world cutthroat.

South Korea's financial change has been especially clear in the gadgets business. Organizations like Samsung and LG Gadgets have secured themselves as worldwide forerunners in purchaser hardware, semiconductor assembling, and show innovation. Their state of the art items are sought after around the world, contributing altogether to South Korea's product figures.

The auto business is another area where South Korean organizations, including Hyundai and Kia, have taken significant steps. These automakers have succeeded in delivering great vehicles, both locally and in worldwide business sectors. Their interests in innovative work, mechanical progressions, and proficient creation processes have made them impressive rivals in the worldwide car industry.

Biotechnology is another region where South Korea has gained critical headway. The country's biotech firms are engaged with historic exploration in fields like genomics, drugs, and regenerative medication. South Korea's commitments to the worldwide battle against the Coronavirus pandemic, including quick testing and immunization improvement, further feature its biotechnological abilities.

Notwithstanding conventional enterprises, South Korea's attention on development and innovation has extended to arising areas like environmentally friendly power and computerized reasoning (simulated intelligence). The public authority's drives to advance green advancements, alongside the combinations' interests in man-made intelligence innovative work, mirror the country's assurance to remain at the cutting edge of mechanical progressions.

Globalization and exchange have permitted South Korea to send out its mechanical items and mastery around the world. The country's capacity to enhance, adjust, and answer worldwide difficulties, especially during the Coronavirus pandemic, has supported its situation as a worldwide innovation and development pioneer. South Korea's combinations, with their different business portfolios, play had a focal impact in driving these commodity triumphs.

The connection among globalization and exchange stretches out past financial aspects. It includes political, social, and social aspects. Globalization has worked with expanded worldwide collaboration, including the arrangement of worldwide associations, economic deals, and discretionary partnerships.

It has advanced social trade, prompting the worldwide notoriety of different social items and patterns. Besides, globalization has permitted individuals to interface, share thoughts, and prepare for social and political causes on a worldwide scale.

The development of global associations like the Unified Countries, World Exchange Association (WTO), and provincial exchange coalitions like the European Association (EU) and the Relationship of Southeast Asian Countries (ASEAN) epitomizes the cooperative part of globalization. These associations act as stages for nations to address worldwide difficulties, arrange economic deals, and lay out conciliatory relations. The WTO, specifically, assumes a critical part in controlling and working with global exchange, setting rules and settling exchange debates.

Economic accords, respective or multilateral, have likewise become fundamental instruments in the globalization of exchange. They expect to decrease exchange hindrances, open up business sectors, and give a structure to worldwide exchange. The multiplication of such arrangements mirrors the acknowledgment that exchange is a strong driver of monetary development and improvement.

Globalization has encouraged social trade and the spread of social items and patterns around the world. The Korean Wave, or "Hallyu," fills in as a convincing illustration of this peculiarity. South Korean music, motion pictures, TV dramatizations, and cooking have acquired huge prominence in different nations. K-popular music, specifically, has caught the worldwide creative mind, with South Korean music specialists and gatherings accomplishing global acknowledgment and fan following.

The worldwide prominence of social items supports trades as well as adds to the travel industry and social strategy. South Korea's social products have created a developing interest in Korean language and culture, with language schools, social focuses, and the travel industry programs taking care of the worldwide interest with Korean culture.

Besides, the computerized age and the web play had a focal impact in interfacing individuals and encouraging worldwide discourse. Virtual entertainment, online discussions, and streaming stages have permitted people to share their thoughts, encounters, and causes with an overall crowd. Developments like the Bedouin Spring and environment activism have bridled the force of computerized network to prepare individuals and promoter for change on a worldwide scale.

While globalization has achieved various advantages, it has additionally raised different difficulties and concerns. Monetary incongruities both inside and between nations have become more articulated. While globalization can set out open doors for financial development, it can likewise intensify pay imbalance, as certain people and locales benefit more than others.

The effect of globalization on business has been a subject of discussion. While expanded exchange and rethinking can set out positions and monetary open doors, they can likewise prompt work relocation and compensation stagnation, especially in enterprises that face global rivalry. The progress to a globalized economy might require retraining and upskilling of the labor force to adjust to changing position markets.

Globalization has likewise raised worries about social homogenization, as the spread of Western social items and values has been seen by some as a danger to neighborhood customs and personalities. Pundits contend that globalization can prompt the strength of a couple of strong social players, restricting variety and independence in social articulation.

Ecological worries are one more huge part of globalization. The expanded development of products and individuals has prompted ecological difficulties, including ozone harming substance emanations from transportation and asset exhaustion. The double-dealing of normal assets to satisfy worldwide need has raised issues of maintainability and natural debasement.

Globalization has additionally achieved changes in political elements and worldwide relations. While it has advanced global participation and strategy, it has additionally prompted political pressures, exchange questions, and difficulties to public sway. Issues connected with monetary reliance and worldwide administration have brought up issues about how nations can keep up with their independence while partaking in a globalized world.

7.1 The interconnectedness of industrial leaders in the global market

The interconnectedness of modern forerunners in the worldwide market is a main quality of the contemporary financial scene. As our reality turns out to be progressively interconnected through exchange, supply chains, and global joint effort, the job of modern pioneers, both worldwide partnerships and provincial goliaths, is more critical than any time in recent memory. This interconnectedness has broad ramifications for the worldwide economy, exchange, innovation move, and the conveyance of monetary power. To comprehend the intricacies and potential open doors introduced by this interconnected trap of modern pioneers, we should investigate its different aspects and suggestions.

At the core of this interconnectedness are worldwide companies (MNCs), frequently alluded to as worldwide players or modern pioneers. MNCs are huge organizations that work in numerous nations, with business exercises spreading over the globe. These organizations have a significant impression in different businesses, including innovation, money, assembling, and administrations, and they essentially impact the worldwide economy.

The ascent of MNCs can be credited to various variables, remembering progresses for transportation and correspondence, ideal exchange strategies, and the globalization of monetary business sectors.

MNCs have utilized these potential chances to lay out a worldwide presence, overseeing creation, conveyance, and promoting exercises across borders. Their capacity to explore worldwide business sectors and supply chains has given them a predominant job in the worldwide monetary scene.

One of the essential elements of modern pioneers, especially MNCs, is to work with worldwide exchange. They act as the key part in the worldwide production network, delivering and disseminating labor and products across borders. MNCs frequently have auxiliary organizations, offshoots, or joint endeavors in numerous nations, permitting them to take advantage of neighborhood markets, access assets, and adjust to fluctuating financial circumstances.

The interconnectedness of modern pioneers stretches out past exchange and envelops unfamiliar direct speculation (FDI). MNCs put resources into unfamiliar business sectors by laying out auxiliaries or getting neighborhood organizations. This FDI animates financial development, innovation move, and occupation creation in have nations. MNCs, thusly, benefit from admittance to new business sectors, assets, and ability.

The appropriation of monetary power in the worldwide market is impacted by modern pioneers and MNCs. These enterprises frequently have significant monetary assets and mechanical capacities, giving them an upper hand. Their worldwide reach permits them to shape market elements, impact exchange arrangements, and lay out industry guidelines. The centralization of force in the possession of a couple of modern pioneers can have both positive and unfortunate results.

On the positive side, modern pioneers drive monetary development and advancement. They put resources into innovative work (Research and development), present new advancements, and make high-esteem occupations. The quest for worldwide seriousness spurs MNCs to remain at the front of development, bringing about headways that benefit society overall.

For example, innovation goliaths like Apple, Google, and Amazon have reformed enterprises and impacted the manner in which individuals live and work. Their worldwide reach and inventive items have reshaped the innovation scene and set new industry guidelines. Their interests in Research and development and constant improvement have prompted the making of state of the art gadgets, programming, and administrations.

Notwithstanding development, modern pioneers fundamentally affect business. They give open positions in numerous nations, adding to pay age and destitution decrease. MNCs frequently lay out assembling offices, research focuses, and administration centers, giving gifted business potential open doors.

On the other side, the grouping of monetary power can prompt worries about monopolistic way of behaving, market strength, and disparity.

Huge partnerships with significant assets might participate in rehearses that smother contest, like savage valuing or hostile to serious consolidations and acquisitions. These activities can restrict customer decisions and block the development of more modest organizations.

Moreover, modern pioneers' worldwide tasks can bring up issues about charge aversion and avoidance. Some MNCs decisively shift benefits to low-burden purviews, limiting their duty liabilities in have nations. This training can lessen the income accessible for public administrations and foundation improvement.

The interconnectedness of modern forerunners in the worldwide market has turned into a subject of discussion and strategy thought. Policymakers and worldwide associations have looked to find some kind of harmony between tackling the advantages of MNCs' exercises while tending to expected negative externalities. Drives pointed toward expanding straightforwardness, upholding against trust guidelines, and checking charge aversion have picked up speed.

While MNCs assume a focal part in the worldwide market, local modern monsters likewise use impressive impact inside their separate circles. These organizations are many times well established in their home districts and stand firm on prevailing footholds in neighborhood markets. The connection among MNCs and territorial modern pioneers is mind boggling, as they can be contenders, colleagues, or even essential accomplices.

China's rise as a worldwide financial force to be reckoned with is exemplified by its provincial modern goliaths and state-possessed undertakings (SOEs). Organizations like Alibaba, Tencent, and Huawei have extended their arrive at past China's boundaries, becoming powerful players in the worldwide innovation and broadcast communications areas. The Chinese government has upheld the internationalization of these organizations, giving them the assets and motivators to contend on a worldwide scale.

In certain occasions, MNCs and provincial modern pioneers might participate in associations or vital unions. These coordinated efforts can take different structures, including joint endeavors, research arrangements, or store network associations. Such associations permit MNCs to get to local mastery and markets while empowering territorial players to profit from MNCs' worldwide assets and organizations.

The innovation area gives a clear illustration of joint effort among MNCs and territorial modern pioneers. Silicon Valley in the US is a worldwide innovation center point, home to various MNCs like Apple, Google, and Facebook. Simultaneously, provincial players like Tesla, Uber, and Airbnb have acquired worldwide conspicuousness, driven by advancement and the sharing economy.

These interconnections stretch out to assembling and creation also. For instance, the car business highlights coordinated efforts between MNCs like General Engines and Toyota and territorial monsters like Volkswagen, BMW, and Toyota. These associations bring about the sharing of innovation, store network coordination, and proficient creation processes.

The connection among MNCs and local modern pioneers highlights the significance of open business sectors and global collaboration.

International alliances and local exchange coalitions, like the European Association and the Exhaustive and Moderate Understanding for Transoceanic Organization (CPTPP), work with coordinated effort and market access. These arrangements decrease exchange obstructions and give an administrative system that upholds the exercises of modern pioneers.

The interconnectedness of modern pioneers isn't restricted to the created world. Arising economies have likewise created their provincial modern goliaths, which have extended their range and impact past their lines. Organizations from arising economies, like South Korea's Samsung, Brazil's JBS, and India's Goodbye Gathering, have become worldwide players in different businesses.

South Korea, specifically, has exhibited the potential for arising economies to create modern pioneers that can contend on a worldwide scale. Samsung, one of South Korea's most noticeable combinations (chaebols), is a prevailing power in the innovation and hardware areas. The organization's capacity to advance, make top notch items, and explore worldwide business sectors has set its situation as a modern chief.

The interconnectedness of modern pioneers additionally reaches out to worldwide money and venture. Monetary organizations and resource the executives firms, including JPMorgan Pursue, BlackRock, and Vanguard, have a significant worldwide impression. They oversee tremendous pools of capital, put resources into different resource classes, and assume a crucial part in worldwide monetary business sectors.

These monetary players have the ability to impact market elements, allot assets, and effect the portion of capital across businesses and areas. The choices made by institutional financial backers and resource directors can shape venture patterns and effect the worldwide allotment of assets.

Globalization has extended the interconnectedness of modern forerunners in the monetary area. Organizations from arising economies, for example, China's Alibaba Gathering and Tencent, have wandered into monetary administrations, including computerized installments and fintech. These organizations have upset conventional monetary models and extended their impact worldwide.

The interconnectedness of modern pioneers has prompted new financial real factors, with suggestions for worldwide relations and strategy. As MNCs and provincial modern monsters extend their impact, they might connect with state run administrations and impact international strategy choices. This communication can be both cooperative, as on account of unfamiliar direct speculation, and ill-disposed, as in questions connected with exchange and market access.

7.2 The role of trade agreements and international trade relations

The job of economic deals and worldwide exchange relations is crucial in the advanced worldwide economy. Economic deals act as the system for monetary connections among nations, molding the standards, duties, and guidelines that oversee worldwide exchange. These arrangements can significantly affect monetary development, market access, and global participation. To comprehend the meaning of economic deals and worldwide exchange relations, we should investigate their different aspects and suggestions.

Economic deals, otherwise called exchange settlements or exchange agrees, are two-sided or multilateral arrangements between nations that specify the agreements of exchange. They oversee the progression of merchandise, administrations, and venture among countries, and they assume a vital part in cultivating monetary combination and collaboration. Economic deals come in different structures, including international alliances (FTAs), customs associations, and financial organization arrangements.

One of the essential elements of economic deals is to lessen exchange obstructions. These hindrances can appear as duties, which are charges forced on imported products, or non-tax boundaries, like amounts, authorizing prerequisites, and specialized principles. Economic accords look to lower or kill these hindrances to upgrade market access and energize the trading of labor and products.

For instance, the North American International alliance (NAFTA), which has been prevailed by the US Mexico-Canada Arrangement (USMCA), brought down exchange obstructions among the US, Mexico, and Canada, working with the progression of labor and products across North America. By disposing of or decreasing levies and non-tax boundaries, economic deals like the USMCA advance a more open and cutthroat market.

The World Exchange Association (WTO) likewise assumes an essential part in managing and working with global exchange. The WTO regulates the authorization of worldwide exchange rules, settle exchange questions, and sets principles for exchange rehearses. Its arrangements cover an extensive variety of exchange issues, including horticulture, administrations, licensed innovation, and exchange related parts of work and the climate.

The interconnectedness of worldwide exchange relations is exemplified by the large number of economic deals in presence today. These arrangements range from reciprocal arrangements between two nations to huge scope multilateral arrangements that incorporate different countries.

The European Association (EU), for example, has a far reaching customs association and single market, taking into consideration the free development of merchandise, administrations, capital, and work among its part states.

Economic accords are intended to help all gatherings included. They set out open doors for monetary development, encourage innovative headways, and improve the intensity of enterprises. By lessening exchange obstructions and empowering the trading of labor and products, economic alliance empower nations to work in what they specialize in and assign assets all the more proficiently.

One of the center standards of global exchange is similar benefit. Nations can deliver specific labor and products more productively and at a lower cost than others. Economic deals work with the specialization of nations here of similar benefit, permitting them to trade their labor and products to different countries while bringing in what they need.

For instance, a country with a relative benefit in farming might trade rural items to different nations, while bringing in made merchandise in which it doesn't practice. This trade of merchandise benefits the two players, as each can get to items at a lower cost than if they were created locally.

Economic accords additionally energize development and mechanical progressions. By advancing rivalry and market access, they boost organizations to put resources into innovative work (Research and development) and work on their items and administrations to remain serious. This drive for advancement prompts the improvement of new innovations and greater products, helping shoppers and enterprises.

Besides, economic deals advance unfamiliar direct speculation (FDI), which includes organizations from one nation laying out auxiliaries, members, or joint endeavors in another country. FDI invigorates financial development, work creation, and the exchange of information and innovation. Global enterprises (MNCs) frequently put resources into unfamiliar business sectors to extend their tasks, access new business sectors, and expand their business.

The connection between economic deals and FDI is frequently commonly supporting. At the point when nations consent to exchange arrangements, they establish a better climate for FDI by diminishing exchange obstructions and giving lawful insurances to unfamiliar financial backers. Simultaneously, FDI can invigorate financial development and occupation creation, prompting expanded shopper interest for unfamiliar labor and products, which further empowers exchange.

Economic deals have not just worked with the trading of labor and products however have likewise assumed an essential part in the globalization of creation. Worldwide worth chains (GVCs) have turned into a characterizing element of the contemporary monetary scene.

GVCs include the discontinuity of creation processes, with various phases of creation happening in various nations.

MNCs have been focal in laying out and overseeing GVCs. They coordinate the different phases of creation across borders, obtaining parts and contributions from various nations and collecting eventual outcomes. This fracture of creation takes into account more noteworthy specialization, cost proficiency, and the development of top notch merchandise.

For instance, the assembling of a cell phone includes various parts and parts delivered in different nations. The gathering of these parts happens in another nation, and the end result is then conveyed worldwide. Economic accords work with the development of these parts and end results, diminishing exchange hindrances and empowering the smooth activity of GVCs.

The effect of economic accords stretches out past financial aspects to international affairs and worldwide relations. Economic accords make strategic ties and cultivate collaboration among countries. The discussion and execution of economic alliance expect nations to cooperate, address contrasts, and assemble common trust.

The European Association (EU) fills in to act as an illustration of how economic accords can add to political mix. The EU started as a typical market for coal and steel in the repercussions of The Second Great War, pointed toward cultivating financial collaboration to forestall further contentions. Over the long haul, the EU developed into a thorough political and monetary association, with a solitary market and a typical cash, the Euro.

The progress of the EU shows the way that monetary mix through economic accords can prompt political and security participation. The EU has turned into a noticeable worldwide player, with a bound together position on different global issues, from exchange and environmental change to international strategy and security.

The job of economic accords and worldwide exchange relations additionally reaches out to issues connected with advancement and neediness decrease. Worldwide exchange can set out open doors for financial development and occupation creation in agricultural nations.

By getting to worldwide business sectors, these nations can grow their products, draw in unfamiliar venture, and take part in worldwide worth chains.

Be that as it may, the connection between economic alliance and advancement is intricate. While global exchange can possibly drive development, it can likewise present difficulties, especially for nations with restricted modern limit or a dependence on a tight scope of products. These nations might battle to contend in the worldwide market, prompting financial weaknesses and pay disparity.

The World Exchange Association (WTO) perceives the significance of tending to the improvement worries of non-industrial nations. It gives exceptional and differential treatment to these countries, permitting them additional opportunity to carry out exchange advancement measures and access specialized help to upgrade their exchange limit.

Economic accords frequently incorporate arrangements connected with specialized help and limit working for agricultural nations. These arrangements expect to assist these countries with partaking actually in worldwide exchange, improve their commodity abilities, and explore exchange rules and guidelines.

Economic alliance likewise raise concerns connected with market access and fair rivalry. A few nations, especially those with huge rural sponsorships and protectionist strategies, may confine market access for sends out from emerging nations. These exchange obstructions can block the development of creating economies and breaking point their admittance to worldwide business sectors.

Furthermore, economic alliance can have suggestions for natural manageability. The trading of labor and products across lines can prompt expanded fossil fuel byproducts from transportation and asset extraction. The overexploitation of regular assets to fulfill worldwide need can raise issues of manageability and ecological corruption.

Be that as it may, some economic accords incorporate natural arrangements pointed toward alleviating these worries. These arrangements look to advance reasonable practices, safeguard imperiled species, and address issues like deforestation and contamination.

Work freedoms are one more basic part of economic alliance. They can have critical ramifications for laborers' freedoms, wages, and working circumstances. Economic accords frequently incorporate work principles that require signatory nations to maintain central work freedoms, including the right to aggregate bartering, safe working circumstances, and the restriction of kid and constrained work.

7.3 The impact of globalization on economic powerhouses

The effect of globalization on monetary forces to be reckoned with has been groundbreaking and multi-layered. Globalization, described by the expanded interconnectedness of nations through exchange, venture, and the trading of data and innovation, has affected the elements of driving economies in different ways. As we dig into the impacts of globalization on financial forces to be reckoned with, it is fundamental to inspect both the open doors and difficulties that have emerged because of this worldwide peculiarity.

Monetary forces to be reckoned with, frequently alluded to as cutting edge economies, are nations with profoundly created modern and mechanical areas, critical worldwide impact, and high per capita pay.

The absolute most unmistakable monetary forces to be reckoned with on the planet incorporate the US, Japan, Germany, the Assembled Realm, and France. These countries have generally been at the cutting edge of worldwide financial and mechanical headways.

The course of globalization significantly affects these financial forces to be reckoned with, reshaping their monetary designs, businesses, and worldwide jobs. One of the essential manners by which globalization has impacted these countries is through expanded exchange and market access. The advancement of exchange, empowered by profession arrangements and the decrease of exchange obstructions, has extended market open doors for financial forces to be reckoned with.

The development of worldwide exchange has permitted these nations to use their upper hands and commodity labor and products to a worldwide client base. For example, the US is a significant exporter of innovation, monetary administrations, and airplane, while Germany is known for its commodities of vehicles and hardware. The expanded network and the launch of business sectors have been fundamental drivers of financial development for these countries.

Globalization has likewise assumed a crucial part in the internationalization of creation. Monetary forces to be reckoned with have progressively participated in worldwide worth chains, dividing the creation cycle and including numerous nations in the assembling of merchandise. This approach has permitted them to enhance creation effectiveness, lessen expenses, and increment seriousness in the worldwide market.

For instance, the development of a cell phone might include the plan of parts in a single country, the assembling of parts in another, and the last get together in one more. By taking advantage of the aptitude and assets of different countries, monetary forces to be reckoned with have had the option to make great items while decreasing creation costs.

The effect of globalization on monetary forces to be reckoned with reaches out to the monetary area. These nations are much of the time home to worldwide monetary focuses, like New York, London, and Tokyo, which assume an essential part in the realm of money. The globalization of monetary business sectors has permitted financial forces to be reckoned with to draw in capital from around the world, making their monetary areas fundamental to the worldwide economy.

Worldwide monetary focuses work with capital streams, speculation, and the allotment of assets across borders. They act as centers for global organizations (MNCs) and financial backers, giving admittance to capital, liquidity, and monetary administrations. The internationalization of monetary business sectors plays upgraded the part of financial forces to be reckoned with in molding worldwide monetary arrangements and guidelines.

Besides, globalization has prompted the internationalization of worldwide enterprises (MNCs) settled in monetary forces to be reckoned with.

These organizations have extended their tasks and market arrive at across the globe, exploiting exchange advancement, market access, and innovation move. MNCs have been instrumental in advancing financial coordination and upgrading the worldwide reach of their nations of origin.

The impact of MNCs from monetary forces to be reckoned with is especially clear in the innovation area. Organizations like Apple, Google, Amazon, and Microsoft, situated in the US, have set worldwide norms for computerized items and administrations. Their mechanical advancements have changed enterprises, affected buyer conduct, and formed the manner in which individuals work and convey.

Japanese organizations like Toyota, Sony, and Panasonic have been pioneers in ventures, for example, car, gadgets, and purchaser hardware. These organizations have made critical commitments to worldwide mechanical headways and play had an essential impact in improving Japan's monetary impact.

The interconnectedness of monetary forces to be reckoned with the worldwide economy has likewise impacted the global work market. Exceptionally talented experts, analysts, and specialists from these countries frequently take part in cross-line versatility, working for global companies, research foundations, and colleges around the world. This versatility has added to the exchange of information and innovation, assisting development and progressions in different fields.

The globalization of the work market has additionally prompted expanded variety in monetary forces to be reckoned with. Foreigners and ostracizes add to the social extravagance and variety of these nations, bringing their abilities, encounters, and points of view to the labor force and society. This variety has encouraged advancement and innovativeness, improving the upper hand of financial forces to be reckoned with.

Monetary forces to be reckoned with have additionally profited from globalization through the inflow of unfamiliar direct speculation (FDI). FDI includes unfamiliar organizations laying out auxiliaries, off-shoots, or joint endeavors in these countries. FDI invigorates monetary development, innovation move, and occupation creation.

For instance, unfamiliar automakers have put resources into assembling offices in the US, adding to monetary development, work creation, and the exchange of assembling advances. Likewise, Japan has drawn in FDI in different businesses, including auto, hardware, and drugs.

The globalization of instruction has been one more road through which financial forces to be reckoned with have benefited. Understudies and researchers from around the world look for training and examination open doors in these nations, drawn by their top notch colleges and exploration establishments. The trading of information and ability has driven advancement and added to the worldwide standing of these countries in the field of schooling.

Financial forces to be reckoned with have likewise assumed an essential part in molding the worldwide administration framework. Their impact in global associations, like the Assembled Countries, the World Exchange Association (WTO), and the Global Financial Asset (IMF), has been significant. They have added to molding worldwide strategies, exchange guidelines, and worldwide monetary steadiness.

In any case, globalization has likewise presented difficulties and intricacies for financial forces to be reckoned with. One of the huge difficulties is monetary rivalry from arising economies. Countries like China, India, Brazil, and South Korea have encountered quick monetary development and have become considerable rivals in different businesses.

For example, China's fast industrialization and commodity situated development have made it a huge player in assembling, hardware, and innovation. Chinese organizations like Huawei and Alibaba have extended their worldwide reach, testing the strength of MNCs from laid out monetary forces to be reckoned with.

The ascent of arising economies has likewise made shifts in world-wide stock chains and creation designs. Financial forces to be reckoned with have needed to adjust to these changes, updating their techniques to stay cutthroat in the worldwide market.

Additionally, globalization has raised worries about the reevaluating of occupations and the effect on homegrown ventures. As financial forces to be reckoned with have taken part in worldwide worth chains and creation organizations, certain enterprises and occupation areas have confronted difficulties, including position uprooting and wage stagnation.

For instance, the reevaluating of blue collar positions to nations with lower work costs an affects modern specialists in monetary forces to be reckoned with. The mechanization of creation processes, driven by innovative headways, has additionally affected work markets.

Moreover, globalization has prompted expanded pay imbalance in a few financial forces to be reckoned with. While globalization can possibly drive financial development and advancement, its advantages have not been similarly circulated. A few people and districts have helped more than others, adding to differences in pay and financial prosperity.

Globalization has likewise introduced difficulties connected with licensed innovation privileges and contest strategy. Financial forces to be reckoned with, as home to persuasive MNCs, have needed to resolve issues like patent encroachments, against serious practices, and market predominance.

The security of protected innovation freedoms is fundamental for MNCs, as it supports their upper hand and development. However, the implementation of these freedoms can prompt questions and pressures, especially when organizations experience difficulties connected with protected innovation robbery in unfamiliar business sectors.

Globalization has additionally brought about issues connected with ecological manageability and asset the executives. The expanded development of products and individuals has prompted ecological difficulties, including fossil fuel byproducts from transportation and asset overexploitation.

To address these difficulties, monetary forces to be reckoned with have progressively centered around manageability, natural guidelines, and capable strategic approaches. They have acquainted measures with lessen their carbon impression and advance the utilization of environmentally friendly power sources.

Globalization has likewise affected social and cultural parts of monetary forces to be reckoned with. The trading of thoughts, data, and social items has advanced social orders, prompting more noteworthy social variety and worldwide availability. Nonetheless, it has likewise raised worries about social homogenization and the strength.

Chapter 8

Challenges and Future Outlook

The difficulties and future standpoint for the worldwide economy are profoundly interconnected, mirroring the mind boggling and dynamic nature of our cutting edge financial scene. In this conversation, we will investigate a portion of the huge difficulties that the world countenances, look at how they connect with each other, and consider expected ways ahead. The future standpoint for the worldwide economy will be molded by these difficulties, with the two amazing open doors and vulnerabilities not too far off.

Financial Imbalance: Perhaps of the most squeezing challenge in the worldwide economy is monetary disparity. Variations in pay and abundance have extended in numerous nations, prompting social turmoil and worries about the reasonableness of the monetary framework. Financial imbalance is a complex issue, driven by elements like innovative headways, globalization, and expense strategies. It influences admittance to training, medical services, and financial open doors. Tending to financial disparity isn't just an ethical objective yet additionally fundamental for social strength and supported monetary development.

Environmental Change and Natural Maintainability: Environmental change is a worldwide emergency with sweeping financial ramifications. Climbing temperatures, outrageous climate occasions, and natural corruption present dangers to ventures, framework, and supply chains. The change to a more supportable and low-carbon economy is fundamental, however it likewise presents monetary difficulties. Offsetting ecological security with monetary development requires creative approaches, green innovations, and worldwide participation. Environmental change transformation and relief techniques are fundamental for building a versatile worldwide economy.

Worldwide Wellbeing Difficulties: The Coronavirus pandemic brought worldwide wellbeing difficulties to the front. Irresistible infections, like pandemics, can possibly disturb economies, strain medical services frameworks, and make vulnerability. The future standpoint incorporates the requirement for further developed worldwide wellbeing foundation, early admonition frameworks, and global collaboration on antibody dispersion and readiness. Wellbeing emergencies can have financial expanding influences, and versatility against such difficulties is essential.

Mechanical Progressions and Robotization: Quick innovative headways, including computerized reasoning and computerization, are changing ventures and the work market. While these advancements can improve efficiency and proficiency, they additionally raise worries about work relocation and changes in the idea of work. Setting up the labor force for the positions representing things to come and resolving issues connected with work freedoms and pay disparity are fundamental parts representing things to come monetary scene.

Exchange Pressures and International Shakiness: Exchange strains and international competitions can possibly upset worldwide exchange, supply chains, and global relations. Continuous debates, like the U.S.-China exchange struggle, highlight the requirement for tact and participation in settling exchange related issues. Exchange wars and protectionist arrangements can prompt financial failures and vulnerability, influencing organizations and customers. Multilateral endeavors to advance free and fair exchange are fundamental for the worldwide economy.

Segment Changes: Segment shifts, for example, maturing populaces and declining rates of birth in many created nations, present difficulties for monetary development and social government assistance. The need to help retired folks, keep a talented labor force, and adjust to changing segment structures requires creative strategies and long haul arranging. Migration strategies, family backing, and interests in schooling and medical care are pivotal for tending to segment difficulties.

Obligation and Monetary Strength: Elevated degrees of government and corporate obligation can present dangers to monetary soundness. Overseeing obligation and forestalling monetary emergencies require reasonable monetary arrangements, straightforward monetary guidelines, and worldwide coordination. The worldwide monetary framework's versatility and capacity to endure shocks, like the 2008 monetary emergency, are fundamental to the future viewpoint of the worldwide economy.

Worldwide Administration and Participation: Powerful worldwide administration and collaboration are essential for tending to shared difficulties. These incorporate issues like environmental change, general wellbeing, and financial solidness. Guaranteeing that global foundations, like the Unified Countries and the World Exchange Association, are good for reason and ready to advance participation is fundamental. Multilateralism and political endeavors will keep on forming the worldwide monetary scene.

Energy Progress: The change to cleaner and more reasonable energy sources is difficult for the worldwide economy. Moving away from non-renewable energy sources and decreasing fossil fuel byproducts is fundamental for battle environmental change. This progress likewise presents open doors for development, work creation, and monetary development in environmentally friendly power areas. Strategies that help clean energy reception and ecological assurance will be instrumental in molding the future standpoint.

Advanced Change and Information Protection: The computerized economy and the assortment of huge measures of information present the two open doors and difficulties. Guaranteeing information security, online protection, and capable information use are fundamental for building trust in the advanced age. Advanced change offers new plans of action and financial efficiencies, however it additionally brings up issues about the convergence of force in tech goliaths and the requirement for administrative structures that offset development with customer security.

These difficulties are interlinked and don't exist in disconnection. For instance, tending to monetary imbalance might require arrangements that think about the effect of mechanical headways on the labor force. Similarly, the progress to a low-carbon economy requires development in innovation and the coordination of worldwide endeavors to battle environmental change. In addition, exchange pressures and international precariousness can influence worldwide stock chains, monetary business sectors, and financial development.

Considering these difficulties, the future standpoint for the worldwide economy is molded by a mix of strategy decisions, mechanical headways, and global collaboration. Here are a few expected headings and contemplations for what's to come:

Reasonable Turn of events: The quest for supportable advancement is fundamental to tending to a significant number of the difficulties. Maintainable advancement objectives (SDGs) envelop monetary, social, and ecological targets. State run administrations, organizations, and common society should cooperate to accomplish these objectives. Policymakers need to incorporate manageability into financial and monetary arrangements, and organizations should take on dependable practices.

Development and Reskilling: Empowering advancement and putting resources into training and reskilling programs is basic for adjusting to mechanical headways. Setting up the labor force for the positions representing things to come, encouraging business venture, and advancing innovative work are fundamental parts of monetary development.

Multilateralism and Discretion: Tact and multilateral participation are vital to tending to worldwide difficulties. Compelling worldwide organizations, question goal components, and worldwide arrangements are fundamental for keeping up with harmony, solidness, and participation in the worldwide economy.

Medical care Versatility: Reinforcing medical services frameworks, building worldwide wellbeing foundation, and guaranteeing impartial admittance to medical care are imperative for tending to wellbeing challenges. Pandemic readiness, early admonition frameworks, and worldwide participation on antibody appropriation are basic parts of worldwide wellbeing strength.

Ecological Stewardship: Natural protection and the progress to a low-carbon economy are key to battling environmental change. Strategies that help clean energy reception, lessen fossil fuel byproducts, and safeguard normal assets are essential to an economical future.

Comprehensive Monetary Development: Comprehensive financial development that tends to pay imbalance is fundamental for social solidness. Moderate assessment approaches, support for weak populaces, and interests in schooling, medical care, and social administrations can assist with spanning the pay hole.

Monetary Security: Guaranteeing monetary soundness and forestalling monetary emergencies require powerful administrative systems, reasonable financial approaches, and worldwide participation. Straightforwardness in monetary business sectors and the versatility of the financial area are fundamental to monetary strength.

Advanced Administration and Information Protection: Compelling administration of the computerized economy and information security is fundamental. Administrative structures should find some kind of harmony among advancement and purchaser assurance. Network protection measures and capable information use rehearses are urgent for keeping up with trust in the computerized age.

Variation and Strength: Building versatility and flexibility to worldwide difficulties, whether they are connected with wellbeing, environment, or financial changes, is pivotal. Creating emergency courses of action, broadening supply chains, and putting resources into exploration and framework are fundamental to strength.

Cooperative Associations: State run administrations, organizations, common society, and worldwide associations should fashion cooperative organizations to address shared difficulties. Public-private associations, industry-drove drives, and worldwide alliances are fundamental for making imaginative arrangements.

The future viewpoint for the worldwide economy is dynamic and molded by the decisions and moves made because of the current difficulties. While the difficulties are significant, they likewise present open doors for positive change, development, and worldwide participation. The way ahead will require aggregate endeavors and a pledge to building a more reasonable, comprehensive, and strong worldwide economy that helps all. By tending to these difficulties with foreknowledge, versatility, and a pledge to shared objectives, the world can explore the intricacies .

8.1 Addressing income inequality and social issues

Pay disparity is a persevering and complex issue that influences social orders across the globe. It alludes to the inconsistent dispersion of pay among people or families, with some acquiring altogether more than others. Pay imbalance can have broad social, monetary, and political results, affecting admittance to training, medical care, and open doors for social portability. In this conversation, we will investigate the causes and outcomes of pay disparity, look at the social issues it causes, and consider expected systems for tending to this diverse test.

Reasons for Money Imbalance

Pay imbalance is driven by a huge number of variables, including monetary, social, and strategy related components. Understanding these causes is pivotal to creating compelling arrangements.

Mechanical Headways: The quick advancement of innovation, especially in the fields of computerization and man-made consciousness, has reshaped the work market. While these advancements can possibly increment efficiency, they can likewise prompt work relocation and pay incongruities. High-talented specialists might profit from innovative progressions, while low-gifted laborers face diminished open positions and stale wages.

Globalization: The globalization of the economy has extended market access and set out open doors for worldwide exchange and venture. Notwithstanding, globalization has likewise prompted work rethinking and rivalry in labor markets. Enterprises and districts that are less aggressive in the worldwide economy might experience the ill effects of employment misfortunes and diminished livelihoods.

Instructive Inconsistencies: Admittance to quality training is a huge determinant of pay disparity. Variations in instructive open doors can prompt contrasts in abilities, capabilities, and procuring potential. Those with restricted admittance to quality schooling face difficulties in getting to more lucrative positions.

Work Market Moves: The idea of work is advancing, with the gig economy and non-standard business courses of action turning out to be more pervasive. Such game plans frequently miss the mark on employer stability, advantages, and compensation securities of customary work. Therefore, laborers in non-standard business might confront pay shakiness and uncertainty.

The lowest pay permitted by law Strategies: The level of the lowest pay permitted by law, where it exists, assumes a part in pay disparity. A low the lowest pay permitted by law can bring about a huge piece of the labor force procuring compensation beneath the destitution line. Expanding the lowest pay permitted by law can assist with lifting low-wage laborers out of neediness and diminish pay imbalance.

Charge Arrangements: Duty approaches, especially those connected with pay and abundance, can either intensify or moderate pay imbalance. Moderate duty frameworks, which charge higher livelihoods at a higher rate, can diminish pay imbalance. On the other hand, backward duty frameworks that put a higher taxation rate on lower-pay people can enlarge the pay hole.

Admittance to Medical services and Advantages: Deficient admittance to medical services and social wellbeing nets can add to pay imbalance. People without admittance to reasonable medical services might confront high clinical expenses, while those without admittance to joblessness benefits or paid family leave might battle during times of financial flimsiness.

Results of Pay Disparity

The results of pay imbalance stretch out past monetary incongruities. Pay disparity has extensive social and monetary impacts, influencing different parts of society:

Wellbeing Variations: Exploration shows that pay imbalance is connected to wellbeing inconsistencies. Individuals with lower wages will quite often have less fortunate wellbeing results, diminished future, and restricted admittance to medical care administrations. Elevated degrees of pay disparity can prompt higher paces of ongoing illnesses, emotional well-being issues, and medical services imbalances.

Training Variations: Pay imbalance can bring about abberations in instructive open doors. Youngsters from low-pay families frequently have restricted admittance to quality schooling, which can influence their scholarly accomplishment and long haul possibilities. Schooling is a critical consider social versatility, and pay imbalance can thwart the vertical portability of distraught people.

Social Portability: Elevated degrees of pay imbalance can smother social versatility. At the point when pay abberations are critical, it turns out to be more provoking for people to climb the financial stepping stool. The absence of social portability can prompt the propagation of destitution and restricted open doors for individual and financial development.

Wrongdoing and Social Turmoil: Pay disparity has been related with higher crime percentages and social distress. At the point when there is a distinct difference between the well off and the ruined, social pressures can heighten, prompting fights, common distress, and even brutality. Decreasing pay disparity is critical for keeping up with social dependability and lessening wrongdoing.

Political Flimsiness: Pay imbalance can impact political elements. At the point when people see that the political and financial frameworks are slanted for the rich, it can disintegrate trust in foundations and lead to political polarization. Tending to pay disparity is fundamental for saving the dependability of popularity based social orders.

Monetary Development: Over the top pay disparity can inconveniently affect financial development. At the point when pay is concentrated among a little piece of the populace, generally speaking buyer request might decline, prompting decreased financial movement. Conversely, a more evenhanded dispersion of pay can prompt higher buyer spending and more noteworthy financial development.

Social Issues Connected with Pay Disparity

Pay disparity is connected to different social issues that have huge ramifications for social orders around the world:

Neediness: Pay imbalance is firmly connected with destitution. Those with lower salaries frequently battle to meet their fundamental necessities, like food, lodging, and medical care. Neediness can bring about unfortunate day to day environments, restricted admittance to training, and compromised wellbeing.

Medical care Variations: Pay imbalance can prompt differences in admittance to medical care administrations. People with lower salaries might confront monetary obstructions to getting important clinical consideration, bringing about inconsistent wellbeing results.

Instructive Disparities: Pay imbalance is a significant supporter of instructive disparities. Kids from low-pay families frequently go to schools with less assets, lower-quality instructing, and decreased extra-curricular open doors. This can bring about lower scholastic accomplishment and restricted admittance to advanced education.

Lodging Instability: Elevated degrees of pay imbalance can prompt lodging weakness. Those with lower salaries might battle to manage the cost of stable lodging, prompting vagrancy or unsafe living plans.

Food Frailty: Pay disparity is connected to food instability, as people with restricted monetary assets might not approach a predictable, nutritious eating routine. Food frailty can prompt hunger and related medical problems.

Social Rejection: Pay disparity can bring about friendly avoidance, with underestimated people and gatherings encountering separation and detachment. Social prohibition can sustain patterns of neediness and limit admittance to amazing open doors.

Procedures to Address Pay Disparity

Tending to pay imbalance is a complex undertaking that requires composed endeavors at different levels, from government strategies to strategic approaches and local area commitment. Here are a few techniques for relieving pay imbalance and its related social issues:

Moderate Tax collection: Carry out moderate expense frameworks that charge higher livelihoods at a higher rate. Changes can expand the taxation rate on the most well off people, giving income to social projects and lessening pay disparity.

The lowest pay permitted by law Expands: Raise the lowest pay permitted by law to furnish low-wage laborers with a more reasonable pay. Normal acclimations to the lowest pay permitted by law can assist keep it in accordance with the average cost for many everyday items.

Admittance to Instruction: Guarantee evenhanded admittance to quality training for all. Putting resources into state funded training, lessening abberations in school financing, and offering help for distraught understudies can work on instructive results and advance social versatility.

Medical services Access: Foster general medical services frameworks or further develop admittance to medical services administrations, lessening monetary obstructions to clinical consideration. Better populaces are better prepared to take part in the labor force and add to financial development.

Social Wellbeing Nets: Reinforce social security nets to offer help for those confronting joblessness, inability, or different difficulties. Sufficient social security nets can assist people and families with enduring monetary vulnerabilities.

Work Preparing and Reskilling: Put resources into work preparing and reskilling projects to furnish laborers with the abilities required for developing businesses. Deep rooted learning can improve employability and professional success.

Specialist Insurances: Execute work strategies that safeguard laborers' privileges, guarantee fair wages, and manage non-standard business game plans. Solid work insurances are pivotal for lessening pay disparity.

Reasonable Lodging: Foster reasonable lodging drives to address lodging weakness. Reasonable lodging projects can give stable everyday environments to people and families.

Nourishment Projects: Extend sustenance projects to battle food uncertainty. These projects can assist with guaranteeing that people approach nutritious food.

Local area Improvement: Advance people group advancement drives that address financial differences at the nearby level. These drives can incorporate work creation, independent venture backing, and local area foundation upgrades.

Corporate Social Obligation: Urge organizations to take on socially capable practices that incorporate fair wages, representative advantages, and moral inventory network the executives. Organizations can assume a part in lessening pay disparity.

8.2 Environmental sustainability and green technologies

Natural supportability has turned into a basic worldwide worry in the 21st 100 years. As the world wrestles with environmental change, asset exhaustion, and ecological corruption, the need to progress toward additional supportable practices is central. Green advancements, enveloping a wide cluster of developments and practices that focus on natural protection, are at the front of this change. In this conversation, we will investigate the difficulties presented by natural maintainability, the job of green advances, and the potential for a more practical future.

Challenges in Ecological Maintainability

Environmental Change: Environmental change is quite possibly of the most squeezing natural test. The expansion in ozone harming substance emanations, fundamentally from the consuming of petroleum products and deforestation, has prompted a dangerous atmospheric devation. This, thusly, brings about additional continuous and serious climate occasions, rising ocean levels, and disturbances to environments. Moderating environmental change is a focal part of natural maintainability.

Asset Exhaustion: The overexploitation of normal assets, including freshwater, woodlands, minerals, and arable land, has overburdened the climate. Consumption of these assets can prompt water shortage, deforestation, soil corruption, and loss of biodiversity. Feasible administration of assets is vital for long haul ecological supportability.

Biodiversity Misfortune: Biodiversity is fundamental for environment versatility and human prosperity. In any case, biodiversity misfortune is happening at a disturbing rate because of environment obliteration, contamination, and environmental change. Safeguarding and moderating biodiversity are fundamental parts of natural maintainability.

Air and Water Contamination: Contamination, whether as air poisons or impurities in water bodies, presents wellbeing dangers to people and biological systems. Hurtful outflows from modern cycles, transportation, and agribusiness add to air contamination, while inappropriate garbage removal and overflow lead to water contamination. Economical practices plan to decrease contamination and safeguard air and water quality.

Squander The board: The age and inappropriate removal of waste, including plastic waste, e-squander, and risky materials, add to natural corruption. Successful waste administration techniques, including reusing, squander decrease, and safe removal, are fundamental for natural manageability.

Sea Wellbeing: Seas are basic for biodiversity, environment guideline, and food sources. Nonetheless, overfishing, contamination, and sea fermentation are undermining the wellbeing of marine environments. Reasonable fisheries the board and endeavors to decrease sea contamination are indispensable for ecological maintainability.

The Job of Green Innovations

Green innovations include a large number of developments and practices that intend to limit their ecological effect and advance manageability. These innovations and practices assume an essential part in tending to the previously mentioned natural difficulties:

Sustainable power: Green advances in the energy area center around the age of environmentally friendly power from sources, for example, sun oriented, wind, hydro, and geothermal power. These sources are supportable, as they don't drain normal assets and produce negligible ozone harming substance outflows. The progress to environmentally friendly power lessens our dependence on non-renewable energy sources and mitigates environmental change.

Energy Productivity: Improving energy effectiveness is a vital part of green innovations. Energy-effective machines, structures, and transportation decrease energy utilization and lower ozone depleting substance discharges. Energy productivity gauges likewise lead to cost reserve funds and more noteworthy financial manageability.

Clean Transportation: The transportation area is a significant supporter of air contamination and ozone harming substance emanations. Green advancements in transportation incorporate electric vehicles, public travel frameworks, and eco-friendly vehicles. These advances mean to diminish emanations and advance practical versatility.

Squander Decrease and Reusing: Green advancements support squander decrease and reusing endeavors. Developments in squander the executives, like waste-to-energy advancements, treating the soil, and reusing frameworks, limit the ecological effect of garbage removal and lessen the stress on landfills.

Supportable Agribusiness: Manageable horticulture rehearses incorporate natural cultivating, crop revolution, and accuracy farming. These techniques intend to diminish the ecological effect of farming, save soil and water assets, and safeguard biodiversity.

Water and Wastewater Treatment: Green advancements in water the board incorporate productive wastewater treatment processes, water reusing, and practical water decontamination frameworks. These advancements assist with monitoring water assets and guarantee admittance to spotless, safe water.

Carbon Catch and Capacity (CCS): CCS innovations catch carbon dioxide outflows from modern cycles and power plants, keeping them from entering the air. These advancements are fundamental for alleviating environmental change.

Shrewd Lattices and Energy Stockpiling: Savvy networks upgrade the effectiveness and unwavering quality of power appropriation, while energy capacity innovations, for example, high level batteries, empower the combination of environmentally friendly power sources into the matrix.

Green Structure Configuration: Green structure innovations focus on energy productivity, manageable materials, and harmless to the ecosystem development rehearses. These plans diminish energy utilization and limit the natural effect of structures.

Preservation and Reclamation: Green advancements support protection endeavors and natural surroundings rebuilding. These practices assist with safeguarding biodiversity and reestablish environments that have been influenced by human exercises.

Advantages of Green Advancements

The reception of green advances offers various advantages that add to ecological maintainability:

Diminished Ecological Effect: Green innovations limit natural debasement by decreasing contamination, moderating assets, and relieving environmental change.

Monetary Open doors: The turn of events and execution of green advancements set out work open doors and animate financial development in manageable areas.

Energy Freedom: The progress to environmentally friendly power sources diminishes reliance on petroleum derivatives and upgrades energy security.

Cost Investment funds: Many green advances lead to cost investment funds for organizations and people through decreased energy utilization and asset proficiency.

Worked on General Wellbeing: Decreased contamination and cleaner air and water add to better general wellbeing results.

Strength: Green innovations upgrade the versatility of biological systems and networks to natural difficulties, for example, outrageous climate occasions and environmental change.

Biodiversity Preservation: Maintainable practices and preservation endeavors safeguard biodiversity and biological systems.

Obstructions to Reception

In spite of the likely advantages of green advancements, a few hindrances to their boundless reception exist:

Cost: A few green innovations have higher forthright expenses, making them less open, particularly for lower-pay people and nations.

Institutional and Administrative Difficulties: Obsolete guidelines, absence of impetuses, and regulatory hindrances can obstruct the reception of green advances.

Absence of Mindfulness: Numerous people and organizations know nothing about the advantages and accessibility of green innovations.

Mechanical Holes: Non-industrial nations might confront innovative holes and miss the mark on foundation expected for the execution of green advancements.

Protection from Change: Opposition from laid out ventures and people who are hesitant to change their practices can obstruct the reception of green advances.

The Way Forward: Natural Manageability and Green Innovations

To progress ecological maintainability and tackle the capability of green advances, a few vital methodologies and contemplations are fundamental:

Strategy Backing: Legislatures assume a significant part in advancing the reception of green advancements through strategies that boost maintainable practices, for example, sustainable power endowments, outflows decreases targets, and duty motivations for energy-proficient innovations.

Training and Mindfulness: Public mindfulness missions and schooling on the advantages of green innovations can encourage more prominent acknowledgment and reception.

Innovative work: Interest in innovative work is basic for propelling green advancements, lessening costs, and extending their pertinence.

Worldwide Coordinated effort: Worldwide collaboration and information sharing can speed up the worldwide change to green innovations and ecological manageability.

Comprehensive Methodologies: Guaranteeing that green advancements are open and reasonable for all pay gatherings and nations is fundamental for worldwide value.

Industry Commitment: Joint effort with enterprises, organizations, and companies to take on maintainable practices and put resources into green advances can drive huge scope change.

Local area Contribution: Nearby people group can be instrumental in supporting for and executing green advances at the grassroots level.

Long haul Vision: Natural maintainability and the reception of green innovations require a drawn out vision and obligation to safeguarding the planet for people in the future.

As the world faces progressively earnest natural difficulties, the job of green advances in advancing manageability couldn't possibly be more significant. With coordinated endeavors at the individual, local area, public, and global levels, it is feasible to progress toward a more maintainable future in which ecological preservation and monetary prosperity remain closely connected. The quest for ecological manageability through the reception of green innovations isn't just a basic for the 21st 100 years yet additionally a pathway to a stronger and agreeable .

8.3 Predictions and challenges for the future of industrial leaders

As the worldwide scene keeps on developing, modern pioneers, including nations and companies, face a large number of difficulties and open doors. The 21st century has achieved huge changes in innovation, exchange, international affairs, and ecological manageability. In this conversation, we will investigate expectations for the fate of modern pioneers and the difficulties they are probably going to experience on their way to progress.

1. **Mechanical Progressions and Development**

   Expectation: Mechanical progressions will keep on molding the fate of modern pioneers. Advancements in man-made reasoning, mechanization, biotechnology, and clean energy are supposed to upset enterprises and drive monetary development.

   Challenges: Tackling the capability of arising advancements requires significant interests in innovative work, as well as adjusting the labor force to oblige these changes. Concerns connected with work relocation and the moral utilization of trend setting innovations should be addressed to guarantee a smooth progress.

2. **Monetary Flexibility and Expansion**

   Forecast: Modern pioneers will zero in on building financial versatility by enhancing their economies. This involves diminishing overreliance on a solitary industry or commodity and venturing into new areas.

   Challenges: Financial enhancement is a mind boggling and long haul process that includes huge interest in foundation, schooling, and labor force improvement. Political and financial interests that favor existing ventures might present protection from expansion endeavors.

3. **Natural Maintainability**

   Expectation: Natural maintainability will turn into a focal concentration for modern pioneers. The criticalness to address environmental change and asset exhaustion will drive the reception of manageable practices and the improvement of green innovations.

   Challenges: Accomplishing natural manageability requires offsetting monetary development with biological obligation. Carrying out strategies and practices that lessen fossil fuel byproducts, save regular assets, and safeguard biodiversity might be met with obstruction from strong interests. Finding some kind of harmony among supportability and monetary development is a mind boggling challenge.

4. **Worldwide Store network Strength**

   Expectation: Modern pioneers will put resources into upgrading the flexibility of worldwide stockpile chains. Examples gained from interruptions, for example, the Coronavirus pandemic have featured the requirement for more hearty and adaptable store network frameworks.

   Challenges: Building tough stockpile chains requires rethinking obtaining, planned operations, and stock administration. It might include extra expenses and intricacies, which organizations and nations should be ready to address.

5. **International Movements**

   Expectation: International elements will keep on developing, with a rebalancing of force and effect on the worldwide stage. New unions and strategic organizations are probably going to arise.

   Challenges: Exploring international relations requires tact, global participation, and flexibility. Monetary pioneers might confront difficulties in keeping up with dependability in an undeniably multipolar world, described by contest between significant powers.

6. **Segment Changes**

   Forecast: Segment shifts, remembering maturing populaces for a few modern pioneers, will impact work markets and social government assistance strategies. Tending to segment changes will be fundamental for supporting monetary development and guaranteeing social strength.

   Challenges: Adjusting to changing socioeconomics includes creating strategies that help retired people, encouraging labor force advancement, and overseeing movement. Addressing the requirements of a maturing populace while empowering family emotionally supportive networks presents strategy challenges.

7. **Exchange Relations and Arrangements**

   Expectation: Exchange relations and arrangements will keep on developing, with an emphasis on fair exchange, manageability, and work privileges. Respective and multilateral economic deals will assume a vital part in forming monetary collaborations.

   Challenges: Arranging economic accords that fulfill assorted interests and address concerns connected with work removal and pay imbalance can challenge. Offsetting monetary collaboration with homegrown interests is a continuous battle for modern pioneers.

8. **Energy Progress**

   Forecast: The change to cleaner and more manageable energy sources will be a focal part representing things to come. Sustainable power advancements and energy productivity estimates will assume an essential part in tending to environmental change.

   Challenges: Moving from petroleum derivatives to clean energy sources requires significant venture, strategy support, and defeating obstruction from occupant energy enterprises. The expense and accessibility of clean energy innovations will be really difficult for modern pioneers.

9. **Advanced Change**

Expectation: The computerized change of businesses and social orders will proceed, with an emphasis on network protection, information security, and computerized administration. Advanced innovations will additionally shape financial exercises and day to day existence.

Challenges: Offsetting mechanical development with protection and security concerns is a fragile test. Controlling advanced stages, guaranteeing information protection, and tending to the computerized partition are intricate assignments for modern pioneers.

10. **General Wellbeing and Pandemic Readiness**

Expectation: General wellbeing and pandemic readiness will stay a need for modern pioneers. The examples gained from the Coronavirus pandemic will drive interests in medical services framework, examination, and global participation.

Challenges: Guaranteeing medical care access, laying out early advance notice frameworks, and working with worldwide immunization circulation require significant assets and global cooperation. Exploring general wellbeing challenges in an interconnected world stances exceptional hardships.

11. **Comprehensive Financial Development**

Expectation: Modern pioneers will take a stab at comprehensive financial development that tends to pay disparity and gives potential chances to all fragments of society. Moderate duty arrangements and social wellbeing nets will be necessary to this work.

Challenges: Handling pay imbalance and advancing comprehensive development includes combative arrangement discussions and possible obstruction from financial elites. Offsetting financial development with social government assistance is a continuous test.

12. **Fiasco Strength and Environment Variation**

Expectation: Debacle versatility and environment variation will acquire noticeable quality as modern pioneers face more regular outrageous climate occasions and environment related difficulties. Interest in framework, calamity readiness, and transformation systems will be fundamental.

Challenges: Supporting environment variation and guaranteeing evenhanded admittance to assets for strength are intricate issues. Modern pioneers should explore the harmony between momentary monetary interests and long haul environment flexibility.

13. **Training and Labor force Improvement**

Expectation: Instruction and labor force improvement will turn out to be progressively basic for modern pioneers. Setting up the labor force for the positions representing things to come, advancing deep rooted learning, and supporting development in training will be needs.

Challenges: Adjusting schooling systems to changing work market requests and encouraging a culture of constant learning are long haul difficulties. Interest in training and tending to differences in access are vital parts of this work.

14. **Social and Cultural Changes**

Expectation: Globalization and mechanical network will keep on molding social and cultural viewpoints. More prominent social variety, network, and worldwide impacts will change social orders.

Challenges: Adjusting the advantages of social trade and globalization with worries about social homogenization and the protection of social legacy is really difficult for modern pioneers.

15. **Ecological Guideline and Capable Strategic approaches**

Expectation: Ecological guidelines and capable strategic approaches will become norm for modern pioneers. Organizations and countries will zero in on decreasing fossil fuel byproducts, moderating regular assets, and advancing moral stockpile chains.

Challenges: Carrying out natural guidelines and capable practices might involve inflated expenses and opposition from enterprises that don't focus on supportability. Finding some kind of harmony between natural obligation and financial development is a key test.

16. **Global Relations and Strategy**

Forecast: Modern pioneers will assume a crucial part in forming global strategy, security, and international strategy. Their activities and choices will impact provincial steadiness and worldwide struggles.

Challenges: Exploring complex worldwide relations, economic deals, and security moves requires tact and the capacity to adjust homegrown and global interests. Financial and political pioneers will confront discretionary difficulties and the requirement for skilled international strategy.

17. **Emergency The board and Worldwide Cooperation**

Expectation: Worldwide emergencies, for example, pandemics and ecological catastrophes, will highlight the meaning of worldwide joint effort and emergency the executives. Modern pioneers will put resources into emergency readiness and collaboration.

Challenges: Getting ready for worldwide emergencies, overseeing assets, and encouraging global participation require significant assets and discretionary endeavors. Building agreement and an organized reaction is a perplexing test in the midst of emergency.

18. **Administration and Political Frameworks**

Forecast: Administration models and political frameworks will develop to adjust to changing cultural necessities and worldwide difficulties. More prominent accentuation on straightforwardness, responsibility, and responsive administration is expected.

Challenges: Transforming administration and political frameworks might confront obstruction from laid out interests. Adjusting the requirement for viable government with the protection of popularity based values .

www.ingramcontent.com/pod-product-compliance
Lightning Source LLC
LaVergne TN
LVHW010334200726
843507LV00010B/1488